Recognized by international critics as an exceptionally brilliant dancer and choreographer, **Patrizia Cerroni** is an extraordinary artist who has dedicated her career to inventing an entirely new choreographic language based on improvisation and interpretation of emotions. Her vital, expressive, spontaneous and passionate creativity crosses artistic boundaries and embraces many artistic genres. She cleverly blends influences from both Eastern (in particular Indian) as well as Western (American) traditions in her performances.

Patrizia has studied classical dance at the National Academy of Dance, Italy, modern dance and American modern dance. She is the founder of the dance company Patrizia Cerroni & I Danzatori Scalzi, and the recipient of many prestigious international awards like the Silver Targa from the President of the Republic of Italy, Carlo Azeglio Ciampi, for her commitment to the training of the young.

She has participated in the most significant international theatres and festivals, including the Seoul Olympics Arts Festival, Gala Italy in New York, Taormina Art, Festival of Spoleto, Umbria Jazz, Teatro Olimpico in Rome, Simón Bolivar in San Paolo, Rome Opera House, Cairo Opera House and Fiume Opera House, and has given more than 2000 performances. In over forty years of her career, Patrizia has trained more than 300 professional dancers and 20 choreographers. Since 2009, she has been practising her own method of movement therapy, which is based on yoga and emotional freedom techniques (EFT), in New York, Rome and India.

About the Translators

Keerti Ramachandra has been a teacher, editor and translator for over forty years. She has edited more than a hundred books of fiction and non-fiction, and translates fiction and non-fiction from Marathi, Hindi, Kannada, Konkani into English.

Rajika Basu has studied Italian for more than fifteen years, first in New York and later as advanced courses in Italian at Stanford University. A marketing professional, she consults with several companies in the Bay Area where she lives with her Italian husband Giuseppe Andreello and son Arturo.

Praise for the Book

"I witnessed the birth and development of this autobiographical work and immediately felt an affinity and affection for Patrizia's ideas and writing, which gained depth as the book progressed.

The book emanates a joy of life and an entirely legitimate pride, I would say, for a life entirely devoted to art to the extent of it being her reason to live. That art, any art, can and perhaps should perform a sort of therapeutic role for human beings is an ancient belief with deep roots in all traditions and cultures. But Patrizia has metabolized this idea to the extent of it being the guiding light of her life and her dealings with others.

Patrizia is an absolutely top-ranking dancer, choreographer, director with formidable experience, but she is also a shaman. She is a person with a desire to measure up and put herself to the test with the firm belief that she is on the right side, the side that exalts beauty, sees art and Eros as the supreme moment, which helps us to protect ourselves from all ills, a panacea which Patrizia's book tells and retells with inexhaustible resolve and energy. And the enthusiasm all this is suffused with reaches readers pure and intact, prompting a desire for and ability to achieve intellectual fullness and spiritual fervour."

Claudio Strinati (art historian)

"Patrizia has an unprecedented courage and she is a genius, we can say, one not understood. This book has completely captivated me. I would love to turn it into a film."

David Zard (music promoter)

"In this 'novel' Patrizia uses the story of her life as a pretext with the result that it is interesting to two types of readers: (1) reader-audiences to whom she offers insights helping them to reflect on their own lives and thoughts in greater depth and (2) reader-artists who draw inspiration from her thoughts and tales, which become tools with which to do and live art."

Dory Zard (artist)

"*Dance Naked Like Truth* is absolutely fascinating. This autobiographical 'confession' explores in depth Patrizia's long journey to bring together the ego and the self, her soul and her body, the spirit and the flesh. A 'rebellious' and creative life between suffering and pleasure, pain and happiness, loneliness and friendship, lives in a completely free body and spirit.

Patrizia has dedicated her life to dance and she has made a substantial contribution to dance in Italy and around the world; she is an icon of Italian culture. In her fascinating insight she appears to be a great friend to herself with whom she shares a magical loneliness while rendering the pleasant nourishment of her friendship to everyone.

According to Patrizia, friendship, dance and music are expression of beauty, an essential human value, our personal salvation. Bringing the ego and the self together, Patrizia shows how the individual ego penetrates our soul and nourishes us with the sense of infinite, whose strength unveils the human fragility and leads us to the essence of God who dwells in us.

This deep dialogue and confrontation between the ego and the self will continue and it is exciting to be part of this magic."

Pietro Vitelli (writer and poet)

Patrizia Cerroni and Massimiliano Martoriati
in Hyde and Eva, 1995,
Teatro Oimpico (Olympic Theatre), Rome

DANCE NAKED LIKE TRUTH

MY UNAPOLOGETIC LIFE

PATRIZIA CERRONI

TRANSLATED BY
KEERTI RAMACHANDRA WITH RAJIKA BASU

Om Books International

First published in 2026 by

Om Books International

Corporate & Editorial Office
A-12, Sector 64, Noida 201 301
Uttar Pradesh, India
Phone: +91 120 477 4100
Email: editorial@ombooks.com
Website: www.ombooksinternational.com

Sales Office
107, Ansari Road, Darya Ganj,
New Delhi 110 002, India
Phone: +91 11 4000 9000
Fax: +91 11 2327 8091
Email: sales@ombooks.com
Website: www.ombooks.com

ISBN: 978-81-19750-64-1

Printed in India

10 9 8 7 6 5 4 3 2 1

To
Guido

*"Dance taught me the soul–body union;
the spiritual path healed my soul and body"*

Contents

Translator's Note

Translating *Dance Naked Like Truth* has been one of the most challenging, demanding and educative experiences of my career as a translator. The project came to me purely by chance and accepting it was an act of bravado. A six-month certificate course in Italian, a couple of Italian-English dictionaries and a thesaurus were not quite adequate to undertake the task, as I learnt very early on.

I am grateful to Rajika Basu for giving me the base translation to work with, and to Patrizia for patiently explaining every shade, nuance, idiomatic expression and the complex concepts over the phone for a couple of hours every night for almost four years, during which I got a sense of her personality, temperament and core beliefs. With her inputs we have arrived at this book.

Every language has its own dharma and one attempts to be true to that dharma in every aspect—lexical, syntactical and, most importantly, supralinguistic features of the language. While undertaking a translation, I keep this principle in mind for I believe my primary responsibility is to the author. I must be true to the voice, tone, spirit and intent of the author, regardless of the languages from which I am translating.

I am faithful to the text. I do not presume to improve it, nor do I wish to appropriate it. Most importantly, I must be true to myself.

If all this comes together harmoniously, my responsibility to the reader, who will spend precious time and good money on the book, will be fulfilled. About what is lost in translation, much has been said, much will continue to be said.

What has been gained? From my experience of translating *Dance Naked Like Truth* are several extremely telling idioms, colloquialisms, phrases, e.g., We split hairs not into four but sixteen! Give someone the "La"! By retaining them, I believe the English language has been enriched.

Since I have been an editor for as long as I have been a translator, I have always told myself, "Do unto others as you would have them do unto you."

I have followed these few principles while working on this translation, and I believe that it will be meaningful and satisfying to anyone who reads it.

Dance Naked Like Truth would not have acquired the strength and depth of the original text if our editor at Om Books International, Jyotsna Mehta, had not gone over it so meticulously and given it the refinement which the original had. Thank you Jyotsna for giving it the final polish.

Keerti Ramachandra

Foreword

This is the story of a woman, an artist, who has spent much of her life in Rome, New York and India, with dance as the centre of her existence.

The book delves into the author's inner life as a child and chronicles her journey as a teenager growing into a woman. Some of her most significant interpersonal encounters are revealed along with glimpses of her romantic life. Her fascinating life makes this a stimulating narrative.

Her obsessive love for dance comes through vividly interwoven with the intimate tale of her life. What is interesting is the spiritual dimension of her being that ties up well with the spiritual traditions of India, which in a way becomes the co-star in this book.

The readers of this book get transported into the heart of dance and music through the author's recounting of her working relationships, events and some very significant tours in her long and illustrious career.

The story's perspective encompasses five aspects of existence: the mental, the physical, the spiritual, the emotional and the unconscious. "Dance is the music you see, music is the dance you hear" is what one realizes as the book unfolds itself. The horizon of the vision extends to the global cultural and artistic landscape, ranging from the 1970s to the contemporary times enriched with anecdotes from different parts of the world.

The final part of the book takes the readers through some profound dimensions of being. It includes an understanding of the emotions which reside deep within. Here the author shares her understanding of the therapeutic and the spiritual tools she has used in her role as an EFT practitioner and healer.

The importance of learning to love oneself if only to achieve an awareness that we are all actually the authors of our own lives is the compelling message of the book.

Sukrita Paul Kumar,
Poet, artist and critic

1

Finding Myself through Dance

Today while I was meditating, what flashed in my mind, dear reader, was the reason why I wrote this book. I want to share my insights and my realizations because I know that reading about me and my experiences will be useful to you. Just as they are precious for me I know they will be for you too.

I believe you might also want to become self-aware and have the interest and the will to explore the five dimensions of "being"— spiritual, emotional, unconscious, mental and physical—that I was able to. I could penetrate them through immersion in music and dance—the twin arts I have dedicated my entire life to.

While I dance I become one with the music, which keeps me going and then I transmute the music into movement. But there is actually more to it than that. The fusion of music and dance expresses the rhythm and harmony of the cosmos. Dance can be expressed in silence too because dance itself is music. Dance is music seen; music is dance heard.

To meditate is to enter the realm of the heart and to stay there with the mind in silence; to be able to hear inspiration. That is the natural state in which an artist dwells.

I declare I am an artist—an expert on whatever is mysterious.

Deep feelings interest me. I have been interested only in the inner world and everything that connects with it, since forever. In this story, with audacity and courage, I will tell you about my worth without being falsely modest. I am not being presumptuous, I am just being myself, sincere and honest.

I have discovered my worth by being humble, working extremely hard and having deep conversations with myself. I have done enormous work within my universe.

I have come to the realization that to succeed you must have the courage to overcome the most arduous challenges of life, especially the inner ones. I have faced my inner enemies and won over them with great effort. Now I recognize my value. Recognizing one's value is the most difficult conquest, don't you think? Hence, I abhor false modesty.

The strength of each person's will to live sets them apart from another. So how intensely do you want to live?

I know that I am beautiful, good and, more than anything else, I am intensely true. I know I am able to see these values in everybody, even in you! Only the crazy, but the really crazy, know how to do that. So why shouldn't I tell you?

All my life I have been told I am a provocateur.

In the beginning we merely see ourselves for how we appear, then we see ourselves beyond the superficial appearance, and in the end we come to perceive and understand ourselves as we really are, enriched after going through the process of self-knowledge. We give to others what we can give to ourselves first, don't we?

The saints in Paradise love those who are brave and true at any cost, and to them they grant success, which is otherwise much more easily attained by making pacts with the devil. I have always made pacts only with angels.

Thanks to my true blue Milanese mother's enthusiasm, I began taking dance lessons at the age of six. She grew up at La Scala Opera House in Milan, where her cousin Rainò was "first dancer" and her father, Luigi, was the master of trombone, with the acclaimed Italian conductor, Toscanini.

My first year of study was sheer torture. We were regularly made to sit on the floor to do some silly movements with our feet and hands. I used to wonder, *Why am I subjected to all these exercises? Is this really dance?* I must have thought of quitting a thousand times.

Fortunately an incident during the end-of-the-year concert stopped me from quitting. We were fifty girls on the stage, and I was in the front row. Once on stage, I was completely focused on my movements, forgetting everything else. I felt joyous, light and a sense of deep satisfaction, with absolutely no fear of judgment.

After the performance, my friends' mothers came backstage, surrounded me, complimented me on my beauty and showered me with praise, "You are born to dance", "You are endowed with real talent". Young and unselfconscious as I was, it completely astonished me. *I had talent!* I had been completely unaware of this fact until then!

This marked my first success. It awakened in me a strong will to go on with what made me feel accepted, admired and free to express myself.

It is critical for children to be encouraged otherwise they won't succeed in their endeavours as adults. If they are disparaged, they may fail.

I remember a few years ago I saw a show by a well-known French choreographer in which the same choreography was danced first by children, then by young professional dancers and at the end by elderly former professional dancers. It was very touching to observe the great difference in the way each of these three groups performed. I was enchanted to see how the children were the most focused, very alert and impeccable. The elderly were the most simpatico because they were having fun, like playing a beautiful game in which they could let themselves go; the young people looked thoroughly professional, and gave performance of a very high standard, as expected. The success I had with my first dance show changed the course of my life. Mine was a talent that could not stand the code of classical dance, its aestheticizing and suppression of freedom and creativity. I realized then that through dance I could express something deeper—my poetry, my purity and my inner beauty.

I was a rebel child. I was shy, with a deep-rooted fear of communication, yet I wanted to break free from the too-structured code so that I could freely convey my emotions. Even though I was young, I understood that dance was a way to express my inner self. The public acclaim came from the fact that I was transmitting my inner being, which in itself became an element of communication, expression and transmission of my sense of life.

Over the years, I have moved from the silly exercises I was made to do to realizing that "being" is more important than "doing", and that was the transgression! I was able to express my inner world in every movement despite the formality of the code. I was able to go beyond the aesthetics of classical dance, to express the poetry within me. To do this through the language of classical dance that truly began to flourish as a distinct and sophisticated art form in the 1600s in the court of King Louis XIV of France, also known as Sun King, was difficult. That period was the most corrupt of all times, rampant with orgies, power games and court intrigues; the dance thus born expressed those perverted elements. It is a dance that represses, compresses, oppresses, distorts, sickens you—it is the contortion and depravity of absolute power.

The dance of the court of the Sun King is a dance against nature. It is human perversion that revels in submitting the body and, by extension, the soul to these perversions. Physiotherapy and modern orthopaedics show that those postures and movements block the energy in the back and the joints, damaging them and the back too. Classical dance invented pointed shoes. The big toe is one of the most erogenous points of the body directly connected to the brain. So dancing on the tips of your toes is like battering your head. I strongly believe that a law should be enacted to ban this type of unhealthy technique.

Every other dance style enhances and multiplies mental interconnections at all levels. By allowing the brain to process several stimuli at once, with multiple dynamics and noises synchronizing in each movement, true dance sharpens the mind.

There are elements of constriction and repression of the body in almost every culture. What I say about classical ballet, I don't even want to call it dance, is comparable to what happened in Western society under the influence of the Christian world, which twisted the original message of Christ. His message has been distorted by the misogynist Church, which has codified and promoted it to repress and oppress, rather than to serve as a guide for freedom and love, through the realization of the joy that resides in the body. In reality, it has fuelled the sense of guilt, fear and sin which attracts punishment from Heaven.

This distortion has resulted in perversion in a large number of cardinals and priests who allegedly become paedophiles. This is not to imply that the human being is distorted, but rather that they are rarely conscious of the harm that comes from the abuse of power.

At the age of twelve, I remember it as if it were yesterday, I was clear that I wanted to become a professional dancer. I asked my dance teacher, Maria Rosa Ferrari, for additional study hours. She was also doing theatre along with her director husband. She did not have the closed mind of the Academy's teachers whom I later met and instantly labelled "potato and broccoli peelers". They took precious time away from their family and household chores, which really was the life they were cut out for, to spend it on teaching dance.

They simply performed gymnastics because they were unable to express their inner drive. Unlike them, Maria Rosa had a passion for theatre because she had learned to interpret action, as an actress would, and was therefore able to convey through her instruction, the act of letting go and abandoning oneself to the creative process.

After many years of private schooling, my mother first tried to enrol me at Silvio d'Amico Academy of Dramatic Arts and the National Dance Academy. It was clear that, like an actress, I had a strong interpretative component to my dancing. But attending two academies would have been too taxing for me. Besides, the schedules clashed. Regretfully, it was decided that I would take the entrance exam for only the National Academy of Dance in Rome.

The founder of the Academy, Jia Ruskaja, was a great lady. She was able to go beyond the surface. She pulsed with life and had a big heart: she was intense, energetic and emotional. You felt that the moment she looked at you she saw and understood you. In the 1940s, she persuaded the regime of the time to provide her the most picturesque place in Rome: a large building on the Aventine hill overlooking the Circus Maximus and the Palatine Hill. Since 1954, the Academy is located in a complex called Castello dei Cesari, dating back to Roman times.

The Academy functioned as a true gynaecium as Jia Ruskaja had forbidden men from attending lessons there, although she hosted the world's best masters and choreographers. It was only in the 1970s that men were allowed to take lessons there. It was a brilliant project, especially if we consider how narrow, bigoted and closed Italy, perhaps the whole world, was at the time.

When I entered the Academy at the age of fourteen, I considered the other students to be like stabled horses for they pulled themselves back in shock and confusion when they saw me perform. Strange, isn't it? Those tightly reined, inflexible horses in boxes mocked and taunted the free horse that roamed the prairie. The fact that I had been accepted into the Academy with full recognition of my years of study outside could perhaps account for their behaviour. Jia Ruskaja's decision in my case was the first in its long history. My peers treated me with contempt because they thought I had been "recommended".

However, they quickly became friends with me after seeing me perform and stood by me every time I revolted against the constant oppression that was being perpetrated on them—not on me—because those teachers simply did not have the courage to scold or correct me! It is my good fortune that I cannot help but speak the truth.

I defended my companions publicly whenever they were insulted in my presence. I even placed my body right in front of them to protect them. Instead of being taught with rigour, dance was taught in that den of supressed vipers with Fascist-style hardness, almost always in a disparaging tone and often even with insults. It is believed that Mao Zedong had once said that you understand people by the way they dance. Well, then, that was really distorted. What a sick world!

I would weep every night when I came home from the Academy, releasing all the tension accumulated during the day. Also, my feet would bleed because of the pointed shoes. My father simply couldn't understand what made me go for these classes. He was incredibly compassionate yet he could not understand me because he had interests different from mine. I felt sad, lonely and totally misunderstood. My mother wasn't with us. Why I will tell you later.

I could not share my feelings with anyone, which in that situation turned into a terrible darkness from which I could only emerge in the joy of dancing.

I was disturbed by the stark contrast between the beauty of the greenery of the Aventine and the ugliness of the people who populated it, trapped in their petty worlds of rivalry, jealousy, envy and aggression, and in their desperate need to excel at all costs. I was deeply saddened and hurt by their insensitivity.

It was such a different world from mine and indeed so different from my family environment. Thanks to my mother's open-mindedness and vision, I had the freedom to create my own rules instead of succumbing to the dull and unimaginative social conventions of the time.

In the midst of all that pain, it just so happened that Carla Fracci and Beppe Menegatti arrived to make a selection of two dancers for a Christmas TV show. Carla was an internationally renowned ballerina and her husband Beppe was her promoter. They chose me from amongst all the students although they knew I was a minor. I did not care much about that experience. It was boring, both for the pointless choreography and the endless breaks between shots, which is deleterious for us athletes who need to warm up their muscles before dancing. Furthermore, the atmosphere of the Roman television studios was very similar to that of the supermarkets, which I absolutely abhor.

Fracci wrapped in scarves and pale pink shawls was constantly changing her shoes of the same colour, which exasperated me. She interrupted the shooting continuously with her "caprices". For someone like me who loved barefoot dancing, this was challenging. Their attitude of complacency and not delving into the deeper truth of things, left me feeling empty and dissatisfied.

Between the ages of fourteen and eighteen, I attended the fifth through eighth courses at the Academy. Every month new masters arrived with a different approach and a different way of communicating which greatly enriched our experience. I studied with Witaly Osinz, Nathalie Grassowska, David Lichine, Nina Vyrubova, Jean Cebron, Juan Corelli, Zarko Prebil, Boris Trailine, of the English, French, Russian schools, all of whom are true artists. Zarko and Vyrubova were teachers of the Russian school. Although they taught the classical technique, they tutored it in a style less unhealthy than the Academy teachers.

I believe the *how* is more important than the *what* of everything you do.

Even today there is a misconception that learning classical ballet is fundamental to the study of dance. But it is not so at all! Other disciplines, much more natural and with healing properties like hatha yoga, provide a more thorough athletic training and preparation for any dance style and even heal the damage done by other techniques.

To my good fortune, Jean Cebron whom I immediately recognized as a great master, taught at the Academy every year I was there. Although he was born in Paris, Jean, an internationally renowned dancer-choreographer, was a citizen of the world.

I saw him dance for the first time at the Teatro Sistina in Rome as a masterful interpreter of the role of Death in the popular ballet *The Green Table* choreographed by the world-renowned Kurt Jooss and Rudolf Laban, founders of Folkwang Universität der Künste in Essen,

Germany. Jean taught there and that is where Pina Bausch, the pioneer of neo-expressionist dance, also danced on his choreographies. These masters developed German expressionism in dance. They developed a system for writing dance as a code, a technique and a language. This was a contemporary style, capable of breaking the patterns of classical ballet. Although the dance was based on improvisation that was similar to Isadora Duncan's, they structured a thought from those movements. If you succeed in fixing what you have created by improvising, you are able to rationalize it and codify it. I don't think it is possible to use dance writing, as one would use music writing or notations because while dancing there are often too many parts of the body moving simultaneously with too many nuances and intensities to be described. It is possible to fix a choreography only through video footage.

I finally found a true master in Jean Cebron. A man of few words, he commanded tremendous respect. An artist of great passion, he was a centred and intense man, severe but kind, always deeply and dramatically suffering. That was how I, as a teenager, perceived him. I fell in love with him as only a disciple can. I was also extremely shy like him and in awe of him, as he was of me, or so I thought. His exotic face, high and full cheekbones, deep piercing green eyes, a rounded wide forehead, large convex mouth, made him appear like a man from a distant Far Eastern country. We were kindred spirits. Anybody who saw me perform to his choreographies said we moved our bodies identically. Jean's dancing awakened my own natural style of dance for the first time because of him. He was indeed the one who left a mark.

Jean Cebron was my guru. In the Indian tradition, the dance is handed down from the guru to the disciple, from body to body, as a means of transmitting the body's or soul's memory, like one spark lighting another. It is a spiritual transmission. I believe that the relationship between the master and his disciple has to do with the exchange of very subtle energy. When the energy of the master awakens you, you find yourself inside his aura. At that precise moment, the movement is lived, bringing to the surface the expression of the profound mystery hidden deep within you.

By stimulating the interiority of the person interpreting it, the master is able to suggest the movement. The movement transmitted by a deep, artistic, symbolic and interior charge, stimulates those same values in the disciple, but only if they are inherent in the disciple. The audience experiences the same impulse even though they are not required to master the art. It is like making love. That is why real dance is naked, like truth.

The end-of-year concert "Nuàge e Fête" featured Cebron's choreographies, which were based on Debussy's music and another extremely distinctive dance inspired by Greek myths with percussion rhythms and extended silences. We learned his technique in class and during rehearsals. Cebron taught us to dance in silence; the only one among the guest masters who made us move following our internal rhythm, without the need for external music.

I love to dance in silence.

At the age of nineteen, I finished my studies in Rome. Following that I started travelling across London, Paris, Amsterdam, looking for new study experiences. I also went to New York to study the techniques of Martha Graham, Alwin Nikolais, Alvin Ailey, Paul Sanazardo and Pearl Lang, and to the wonderful school of Merce Cunningham, which had a huge studio with windows on two sides that looked out onto the terraces of a West Side skyscraper.

Since I first saw Cunningham perform with his company at the Teatro La Fenice in Venice, I have regarded him as one of the greatest choreographers of all time, and he continues to be, in my opinion, the greatest master of American modern dance. For this reason, I went with the intention of studying everything I could from him. He was fundamental to my growth just like Cebron. Thin and nervous, with curly hair like a mad scientist, he was very similar to Cebron in his attitude. In Italy, Cunningham was widely regarded as a genius recognized by all. I had also seen him perform with John Cage at the Sistine Theatre in Rome seamlessly blending dance and music.

I consider Cunningham's dance to be truly intelligent, as the Latin word "intelligere" suggests, which means understanding interrelatedness. His dance synchronizes the dancers by simultaneously moving various body parts and choreographing the use of the space between them in infinite dynamics.

Cunningham is a genius who has offered directions to future generations through abstract art, linearity and pure mathematics. It could be characterized as anti-erotic, but this is not true because eroticism is inherent when the poetic dimension arises. Eroticism and sensuality are not the same thing; language can be sensual without being erotic, and vice versa. Eroticism and sensuality are two different aspects. Eroticism involves a deeper dimension, comes from the root of the emotions. That is why I believe that eroticism is all about intensity and energy, something invisible. Sensuality appears in the physical dimension.

I was aware back then, as I am now, that mathematics is present in all forms of art, regardless of the style in which it is expressed.

Cunningham's is a cold dance, with expressionless faces and linear bodies. Even though his language of dance was so different from mine, I loved it. His dance resonates with my most intimate and deep sense of being. When the artist goes beyond technique and language, it is pure dance.

Each style of contemporary dance takes its name from the choreographer who created it; each choreographer develops a distinct style and technique that is easily identifiable. Cunningham's technique stands out because it is minimalist, severe and rigorous.

The word "choreography" comes from the word "to write the movements of bodies in space". The body can move only one or many parts of itself and Cunningham was able to synchronize the movements within the body in a unique way. Even if I approach it in a different way than he suggests, for mine is emotional and symbolic, I am grateful to Merce Cunningham for helping me to elaborate on the synchronization of numerous bodily components.

I was lucky that at nineteen my English was not evolved as it is today. I misunderstood what they told me when I went to enrol in his school. I attended what I thought was my class and found myself in the front row of Cunningham's lecture. He did not allow entry to those who were not his dancers. But I continued to attend them for six months without anyone objecting to it. Cunningham let me study as if I were one of his dancers, correcting me and taking care of my movements. I was so fully integrated that nobody had anything to say about my presence among them. I felt happy being in the right place at the right time with the right people. Cunningham left a lasting impression on me and enriched my life. I feel I "stole" much of his genius. We steal from true masters. But this beautiful experience was actually a gift. Thank you, Merce! How I adore you.

Jean awakened my natural dancing style, but Cunningham enriched it with technical, dynamic and choreographic elements. Awakening is different from enrichment. Both Merce Cunningham and Jean Cebron have greatly influenced me.

What makes an artist?

The inspiration that the artist receives tends to plunge into her unconscious depths, where intuition, will, emotion, instinct and the roots of being reside.

The body in its natural integrity is naked. We use the body as an instrument of the soul to create music. Different arts are assembled and synthesized in their totality in dance and in all the five dimensions of being. Dance therefore is the most complete of all arts.

Each artist engages with the spiritual, the emotional, the unconscious and the mental dimension.

The dancer adds the physical dimension to art. The body being its instrument.

What is higher than the sound you see but can't hear?

What is higher than the sound that lives through silence?

What is more intense than silence for sound, and stillness for movement?

The energy that a dancer will release later in the movement is not as great as the energy of her stillness. It is the tension of creative energy before the explosion.

The pioneer of Eurythmy, an expressive dance movement, Rudolf Steiner said that dance is the art of the future and that humanity is not yet able to understand it. It will do so when telepathic and bodily communication becomes commonplace in the distant future, eliminating the need for words.

Seen in this light, dance is presented as a radical, total and absolute experience. That is how I live it.

2

Early Loves

I have intuitively known since I was a child that a man loves a woman and her body while the woman loves his love. As an adult, I acquired a full awareness of this difference.

My papa was my first great love. During my childhood, I would be waiting for him all day yearning for the moment when I would be with him at last. Every evening, Lilla, my blind Jack Russell terrier and I would eagerly wait at the door to welcome him. The moment Lilla would hear his car enter the garage, she would jump around barking, her tail wagging, while I stood there holding my breath, with his slippers in my hand.

As soon as Papa Alfredo would enter the house, I would find myself wrapped around him. After supper we would settle on the sofa, with my arms still around him, tenderly melting into his chest, as we watched the popular show *Caroselli* and then I was sent off to bed. My mamma would have to get up in the middle of the night to cover me, and I would get up to cover Lilla.

My love for my papa was the love of a woman who totally trusted her man. As a child, I imagined I would marry him when I grew up. I believed Papa—a true Roman, tall, handsome, generous, humane and wise would be the only man in my life. Generosity and nobility were innate to my father. Life should be a competition for who can offer more of these. I had never seen anyone being allowed to pay for anything while he was around. I took this kind of humanity from him and carried it to the depths of my being.

My father was a pioneer; he became a tax consultant, a profession which at that time did not exist in Italy. He was amiable and open, and had many industrialists and show-business celebrities as clients.

There was tenderness and a deep sense of mutual trust in our relationship. Children are more capable of such profound feelings. In their simplicity, they live intensely and directly without any filters or barriers.

I was giving him the quality of love he needed, the same kind that he was giving me. We had something unique and exclusive between us.

With my mother, he often had quarrels; he was from Rome, easy-going, laid back and carefree, and she was from Milan, strong, efficient and very practical. I can say that I actually experienced the Rome-Milan conflict. This is why probably he found himself a lover.

One day when I was at the school of the Ursulines Sisters, standing in front of a large window overlooking Via Livorno, during playtime, a classmate told me that my papa had been seen with a blonde woman. My whole world collapsed around me. I felt myself sinking into an abyss of pain from which I knew I would not easily emerge.

I was not enough for him?

I began to alienate myself from playing with other children, and suffered a sense of anguish and profound isolation that was overcome only by taking the first dance lessons. Indeed, Papa had every right to live his life the way he wished to. It was not as if he was betraying me, but I reacted as if he was because no one came forward to explain this to me.

Shouldn't parents explain and reassure their children about such things?

My initial passion for my father was reflected in the intensity of everything I did in my life. I realize now that everything happens for the best. I was driven to dance and the amazing life I had built for myself because of my deep disappointment with what I perceived to be a betrayal.

In order to realize oneself, one must have the courage to risk being free. That is how it should be. Love can be experienced only in freedom because freedom transcends possession.

My father's so-called betrayal has irreparably impacted the relationships I would have with men as an adult. For too long a time my attitude was to present myself only seductively. That has been my way to react to that pain—*giocandomi tutto*, risking everything.

Seduction was the focus of my ten-year, three-sessions-per-week adventure in Jungian psychotherapy, and I now see myself as an authority on the topic.

Seduction is avoiding the risk of getting really involved. In the rather perverted game of seduction we create the illusion of love in order to avoid disappointment. It all starts with the fear of suffering for love. It is just like the snake that bites its tail. We play ahead of the game. It is an unintentional game of slaughter, of punishment for oneself and punishment for the other. In a way this draws boundaries around love, and creates a world in which we don't value ourselves enough to feel we deserve unlimited love, from within ourselves and from others.

It is incredible how children, just like artists, have a direct relationship with truth—through instinctive emotions and intuition, with the same direct, naked and raw intensity. This is why they need continuous and adequate assurance regarding their unceasing demand for respect and love. They need their value to be always recognized and to be addressed without reproaches, punishments and denigrations, even if parents use these measures to diminish their weaknesses and enhance their strengths. It is by encouraging their inherent qualities that the gaps can be filled. If their value is denied, these weaknesses will become chasms that will remain unbridgeable for the rest of their lives.

As adults, they will need to find a good, but really good "healer" who will guide them in rediscovering their own "self-care", which is nothing but love for themselves. It is only from within that this extreme need for love can be filled. Nothing from outside can do it.

We are each born with our own unique nature which is subsequently put to the test by life's experiences and challenges. Our reactions to events create our destiny and often cause distortions in our original nature, leading to unpleasant circumstances. Until we face them, process them and solve them, we continue to create more and more suffering.

By observing people's lives, we can identify the inconsistencies and contradictions between their true nature and the circumstances in which they live. Every human being needs serenity, trust and harmony. Every human being also needs to be treated with gentleness, kindness and sensitivity. This is fundamental for our well-being. We must endure sorrow in order to attain this freedom to be who we are.

So eventually my parents separated. Mamma felt Papa was to blame so like a good car driver, she accelerated in the middle of the curve, and walked out of the house before he could. She feared that he would abandon us and not support us so she left me with him to make sure he would take care of me. But I knew Papa would never have done that. By leaving me with him, she had sold me.

My mother's inability to love my father with the full responsibility of a woman who understood how to be a guide for the man in the art to loving her was the main cause behind their separation. I was able to do this instinctively with my father while she was too busy with her own inner tangles. To truly love, one must first resolve all inner conflicts.

When our actions do not originate in love, power comes into play. It is always one or the other. When Mamma left us she used power, which is the exact opposite of love. She left me at the mercy of her power. I found love only in dance.

From her point of view, she had been very clever by adopting offence as the best form of defence. Her actions unleashed in me a profound desire to reject both her and those feminine dynamics. I would never have done what she did. I would have acted maybe in an even worse manner, more directly, like a man. And so I did. I stopped talking to her and resumed talking to her only thirty years later. Poor Bruna, my mamma.

Mamma had lost her own mother at the age of eight. My maternal grandfather was a musician at the Scala of Milan. He believed that he could not look after Mamma because he was often on the road, so he put her in a boarding school after she lost her mother. Her decision to travel from Milan to Rome at the age of twenty was extremely brave at the time. After the war, she worked alone in Rome at the Center of Italian Fashion, where she rose to the position of director of the tailoring company. Brave Bruna.

When I was a child, Mamma would often cry on my shoulder, and I cried with her, trying to share her pain. It was obvious that the cause for all this was Papa. Once, in a moment of madness, she told me, "If only you knew what your father did!"

In my experience, there is nothing worse for a child to be told something and then not have it explained. I thought, *Has Papa killed someone?* In that way, she was moulding me to stay free from all attachments. Many years later, she told me that her remark referred to something I already knew—Papa had been married when he met her. No wonder my schoolmates looked at me strangely—my parents were not married! It was not very common at that time.

There was also something more. She had interiorized her own father's inability to take care of her after his wife's death as an abandonment. From then on she lost all faith in men. She often told me that one could not trust men as they abandoned you in moments of difficulty.

Papa, exasperated by her never-ending suspicion and mistrust, was driven to find himself a lover.

Despite my circumstances, I was certain that I would be able to overcome suffering, and help other children do the same. To do so, I would become a psychotherapist when I grew up.

I remember once we were driving by Lake Anguillara where we often went for Sunday lunch. There was an underlying tension between my parents; it was then a powerful thought crossed my mind: *I will never become a mother if first I have not resolved pains, conflicts, fears that are building up inside me. I don't want to load them on my children as my mother is doing on me.*

Watching the sky from the terrace of our house in Viale Libia, I used to often ask myself: *Where are we coming from? Where are we going? What is the sense of this existence? Why is there so much sorrow in this world?* I couldn't find the answers to my questions in the immensity of the sky. Not even the Ursuline Sisters knew how to answer these. They used to send me to study Catechism. I found all the pointless doctrines and meaningless symbols with no spiritual significance irrelevant and boring.

Even at the Mass and confessions, I didn't find answers, but only formal expressions of the Divine that I simply could not relate to. But I knew that as an adult I would find the answers, and that confidence helped me to survive. Deep down I knew that I would find them in the Orient.

Mamma was confined to a wheelchair in the last years of her illness. Since I was with her all the time, we became close. To my great delight and satisfaction, I had become her mother then. I was at her bedside at the time of her last breath.

Everyone remembers Mamma as a symbol of strength and tenderness, dignity and generosity, elegance and courage, beauty and goodness. Everybody recognized her vitality, energy and fortitude—all characteristics of a true Piscean. She could be intransigent, capricious and rebellious like a child, but she was also creative and intuitive. It was she who taught me to "play" freely and independently. "Everything is possible" is the message she gave me.

The real hero is the one who resists. She always rose from the ashes, making me proud and honoured to be her daughter.

Given her strong and complex personality, I felt that I had succeeded in riding the tiger. In my dreams now, I often take her with me on the crossbar of my bicycle or on my shoulders, just like the legendary hero Aeneis when he saved his father by carrying him out of Troy on his shoulders.

We are God's characters on the splendid stage of life. Every soul continues to mature in the afterlife before reincarnating in different bodies. Beyond good and evil, the experience of the recently completed life, which was elaborated in the other dimension, would enhance the soul's ability to better understand the role it will play in a future "career" in eternity. The most evolved souls are those who understand evil and know how to protect themselves from it through awareness and detachment. I hope to be able to do so in this life. I am sure I still have a good deal of time left to learn to do it without having to attack it and fight it. We are ourselves responsible for how we decide to experience and react to the outside world with the required distance.

When I was fourteen, Claudio Francisci, a champion racer and the son of a friend of my father's, taught me how to drive a Fireball on the Autodromo di Vallelunga Piero Taruffi racetrack. Even today I am a sporty driver. What was the most precious secret I learned? Accelerate in the middle of the curve. Always raise the stakes in life as well. I was the first girl in Rome to own a Vespa 50. I felt liberated. I felt I owned the city.

As I was blooming into womanhood, the gaze of men gave me a new awareness of myself. I became the mascot of the nightclubs in Rome. I frequented Lo Scarabocchio, the Number One and the Piper to dance away the night. As I was dancing, I was unleashing myself and through improvisation, discovering my real dance. It was the perfect setting to find my own language of movement.

My father was never at home. He would arrive late at night and leave early in the morning. Between school and the Academy I was busy twelve hours a day. But hurting and transgressing, I was self-righteous in my suffering. I also returned late at night, stuffing newspapers under my vest to protect myself from the cold as I rode home on my Vespa. I felt "cool" leading such an audacious life! Part of this was smoking forty Marlboro or HB cigarettes a day. But I was a good girl.

One day, Papa confronted me and reprimanded me for my night outings. He should not have done that. I shouted, "How can you exert any authority over me after the example you have set?" We had a heated quarrel which ended with him slapping me, for the first and the last time in my life! This upset Papa and he started weeping in front of me. I stopped talking to him after that. Forever. He made futile attempts to buy me presents, but my love and self-respect were not for sale. However, since I was not financially independent at the age of fourteen, I merely accepted the bare minimum from him.

He would often say that I was brutally honest and that would create many a problem in my life. Papa Alfredo loved life and had great ability to adapt to changes and new situations. He was very romantic, and loved women. I thought Papa had had enough of them ever since Mamma left home but was always looking for true love which he could never find.

Suddenly, one night in 1974, Papa Alfredo died of a heart attack while in the company of a twenty-year-old girl. Many people think that this is one of the best deaths. I would rather die while dreaming.

Some of my fondest memories are of summertime at Circeo! We would spend our holidays at Hotel Carillon, today Hotel Circe, located at the centre of the promenade. It was a meeting place for us young people.

I used to go to dance till dawn at Chez Nina, the Bussola and the Stiva where various groups performed, including the popular Italian beat band Equipe 84. My admirers were systematically sent away 'empty handed'. This was because of that profound malaise of not being able to trust men, of which I have already spoken. I fell in love with Silvio, a refined and athletic young man with gentle green eyes who captured my heart. He had a villa on Circeo Mountain and we used to go swimming in Punta Rossa. He too had a dinghy like mine, an Attack with a yellow tip and a 35-Cavalli Mercury engine. One night, after the usual nightclub hopping, he escorted me home. He was on his Gilera motorcycle, and I was behind him on my Vespa. I started doing acrobatics on it on the rough gravelly beach road. And guess what happened? I found myself in the hospital with third-degree lacerations on my arms and legs.

And Silvio walked out of my life.

I soon began to understand that the equation between me and love, or rather falling in love, would not be easy. When in love, I tend to show off and then I end up hurting myself. Perhaps it is something we all do deep down. But let me tell you, I don't do it anymore, as I am finally able to love without being narcissistic.

I met Giorgio at a party at the Famija Piemontèisa, an elite club. He was twenty-eight, a graduate in engineering, and already a man of the world, with businesses in London and India. The son of an Alitalia pilot, he would take me flying over Rome from the Urbe airport. In the evening, Giorgio used to drive right across Rome to pick me up from the Academy and take me to his home. In their villa at Eur, he had created an alcove in the playroom with intriguing lights and red furnishings. At that time, at the age of eighteen, I decided to come to the table and bite with my beautiful teeth, the bread that I had been offered from the age of fourteen but resisted all this while. And there began our erotic practices, the first of my life. My dancing become even more passionate. I experienced my body in a deeper way. I lived it then more from the inside.

Sometimes Giorgio would take me to London, for shopping and a tour of the night clubs. Everybody there knew him and welcomed him with open arms as they would a playboy. I loved London and its style.

I was sure that despite being very much in love with me he was enjoying himself with others on his numerous and regular trips abroad. That is why I left him. He followed me day and night for two years after that, disguised behind dark glasses and a long, black beard. The friends who went out with me were scared of this man following us. I relished the sense of vengeance that came with leaving him.

After this episode with Giorgio, there were two possibilities: I either fall in love without living the story in reality or I build stories with those I only liked. It is too risky to do the two together; endless suffering is guaranteed. Not that I have not suffered anyway. I have not seen anyone suffer so much for love as I have—so many times and on so many occasions. In fact, after entering a relationship, I got so involved that I triggered the classic need for absolute love, with its attendant and related torment.

Every human being aspires to happiness by losing oneself in nothing else but absolute love; the only way to find oneself. That is what I feel when I dance.

So how did I seduce them? I fed them with the illusion of love, I released my sensuality and sweetness in a sinuous way, and with a lot of humour and sarcasm. I challenged men on the level of their intelligence.

I met Giorgio again a few years ago and he took me from Rome to Florence for lunch on his private airplane. He was a very successful, internationally known and extremely wealthy businessman. He confessed to me then that he never ever felt as loved by anyone as by me, and he had always been afraid that he could never win over my dance. All of us human beings need to be in the first row and have exclusivity in the lives of those we think we love. I was not really in love with Giorgio. I would not have been able to stay with him if I had been.

He confided in me about his problems with his first American wife, who returned to the US and didn't want him to even meet their son anymore. He also discussed his issues with the present Russian wife, much younger than him, with whom he had other children. Problems will undoubtedly keep coming up in different ways if they are not fixed at their core. My mother liked him very much, but never as much as she liked Guido; more about him later.

The next person in my life was Corrado. A short anecdote to understand the type. I was told by a psychic on my first trip to India that

I was much envied, and oddly enough, particularly by men. In particular, he visualized a dark man with a long nose. This is exactly what Corrado, a recent graduate in architecture, was. He does not deserve too much attention, but like Giorgio he connected me to India. He dressed only in black, had a sinister charm which was irresistible, yet he was a blot in my life. He was a fake guru and a highly cultured man who captivated people with his seeming wisdom and expertise. A misogynist, he used me to understand how I could be a woman and a dancer, depriving me of the joy of using my body to express myself because his own was entirely suppressed by the jealousy and hatred he harboured within. Repression produces monsters.

Since I didn't choose him but rather decided to become a choreographer, Corrado encouraged me to continue my craft despite the fact that years later he would criticize me for it, as genuine plagiarists and deranged manipulators do. I am glad I chose dance over him; I consider this as my best and wisest decision. As a dancer I felt the anguish of having been robbed of my enthusiasm, my joy and my creativity which go to make me a person of great vitality. When he finally left, I found myself at Papa's house, shattered and depressed, cloistering myself for months in a dark room.

Probably at that moment in my life I needed to learn how to reinforce "weak muscles" and deal with negative persons. The vampire had sucked all my energy. I can say that he had used me.

Mediocre architects love black.

Both Giorgio and Corrado realized that they could not compete with my dance because no matter what, that would always be my first love. Difficult to bear for ordinary men.

To my great good fortune I finally met a special man, the architect Guido Paolo Menocci.

3

Gentle Giant Guido

He stood out above everyone else. There was a fire always burning inside him. He was an eagle when he was flying and a pure white swan when he was gliding over the ground. Just like the swan in the water, he displayed his dignity with humility. Guido was able to love me in a way that was absolute, and stayed close to me forever.

He loved both me and my dance instantly. He gave everything he had—his skills, his poems, his whole self and more—to us. And my dance and I became the meaning of his life. It was a great honour for me and my art.

Guido was the most important and the dearest person in my life; the one I loved and respected the most. Ours was a great love, which I turned into friendship—which I think is the highest of human relationships—with his help, of course. I was always faithful to this friendship and it remains the most genuine and unique in my life.

It was clear that I loved him in a different way than he did—so human, that I seemed inhuman. I have always had a basic need for total freedom. I could love only in freedom. Of course, Guido suffered because of this, although he claimed that it was worth it. He once said, "One always gains more in the exchange with you." That meant a lot to me though I don't know how much of that was true.

Like my father, Guido was generous and protective, and a true Cancerian. He made me feel I could trust him and rely on him to let me be free. This is love; you cannot fill your own emptiness through the love of another person. Loving is sharing of "fullness". Dance became the cement of our love.

During the historic year of the European student movement in 1968, Guido was part of the well-known and avant-garde group of undergraduates, Gli Uccelli (The Birds) at the Faculty of Architecture of Valle Giulia. They stood out within the student movement by organizing extraordinary activities rather than taking part in the customary protests. The group went also to visit the intellectuals and artists of that age, to paint the walls of their homes with fantastic images that were talked about in the media. It was an honour to have been chosen by them.

The group first began to live together in Viale Parioli, and then in Via Rubicone, as guests of Claudio Del Vecchio, a cultured dentist, who offered them his apartment. They became a kind of beacon for all of us young people. The slogan "Imagination in Power" was created by this generation. Regretfully, despite Guido being one of the key founding members of the group, they neglected to even mention his name in a recent video celebrating The Birds. What narcissism and egocentrism!

When I met Guido in 1971, he was already a successful architect and a founding partner of one of the most prestigious studios in Rome, Technark Italia. He had completed significant projects, including whole neighbourhoods like Spinaceto and Vigna Murata.

He was immensely moved when he saw my choreography of "Marche!" on Igor Stravinsky's *L' Histoire du Soldat* (The Tale of a Soldier) for the first time during the performance at the school where I was teaching. He later told me, "I was so completely absorbed in it that I found myself chewing on my cigarette."

Given his great sensitivity and sophistication, I could see why he was greatly impressed by "Marche!"

I had created it earlier in the Academy, which was performed here by Loredana, a ten-year-old student of mine, athletic, muscular and linear, with impeccable technique which was perfect for the piece. In order to parody classical ballet, which was later performed by male dancers, I had created it for a man on the tips of his toes. Here movements are always angular and rigid and broken as they divide each part of the body while synchronizing them in different directions. "Brilliant and perfect for that music!" is what I can say without hesitation.

Guido recognized all kinds of value immediately. He once told me, "True culture lies in sensitivity." Because of his love for me he also became an expert in dance and played an important part in establishing my modern dance company.

Patrizia Cerroni e I Danzatori Scalzi (Patrizia Cerroni & the Barefoot Dancers) was founded in 1974 in Vicolo del Babuccio, our studio, being a few steps from the famous eighteenth-century Fontana di Trevi (Trevi Fountain). The only reason I could start the company was because I had Guido, a man of great worth and strength, by my side. I could never have created it in Italy by myself.

I recall how the name of the company was born through a game of "four hands" we played while lying in bed. As we began brainstorming on potential names, Guido suggested "The dancers", and then after a long list of names "*scalzi* (barefoot)", which sounded perfect in both sound and meaning and was symbolic as well—it came out of the hat as if by magic.

Did you know that at the entrance of Indian temples, it is often written "Leave outside your ego with your shoes"? Guido learned that there were barefoot doctors in China who treated the poor in the countryside.

Guido's presence in my life has been vital in every sense. If I were to relive my life I would do everything I did with him all over again. When I had the opportunity to relocate to New York, I decided to stay in Rome with Guido, the *core* of my existence.

Guido was a good and gentle giant who was strong enough to resist all travails of life. I once saw him, two metres tall and with the shoulders of an athlete, hoisting a massive wardrobe from the Renaissance era and shifting it from one wall to another with just a lever. He looked like one of those biblical figures depicted in the Sistine Chapel. He won the hearts of many women; after all, he was the ideal man.

While I was in India, Alarmel Valli, a beautiful and well-known Indian dancer met him when she came to perform at the Olympic theatre in Rome. "I envy you only one thing—Guido," she later told me. He was lovely, kind, with warm green eyes, tender but solemn and severe. He was both paternal and maternal to everyone, filling one with warm affection. He gave one the confidence to be oneself and to follow one's natural movements just like when one is in water. You could trust him blindly and entrust yourself to him. Everyone felt protected in his presence because Guido was a wise, clear-headed man with a unique and rare sense of fairness and ethics.

He was light years ahead of others in technology, and he could build computers, like anything else, with his great Michelangelo hands. For me Guido was a sort of Leonardo da Vinci because he had exceptional abilities in almost every field. Always very curious, always active and ever creative, Guido had extensive knowledge in a variety of fields. I don't think I have ever met a person more well-informed and cultured than him. He knew everything about painting, sculpture, art history, architecture, cinema and literature. His understanding and knowledge of music was on par with the best musicologists. He loved all the arts and he was truly creative in graphics and design. He was also an exceptionally good cartoonist, with a style reminiscent of the legendary Guido Crepax. After our tour, he produced brochures for the ministry using pictures and graphics that were so stunning that they astounded the government officials. True masterpieces!

As an administrator, he had the wisdom and the knowledge to find answers to legal problems too. As an artist with exceptional perception, he supported and fostered others' creativity with great empathy. Something very rare. It is remarkable that despite all his talents and skills, he was neither egocentric nor narcissistic. His sensitivity, which he offered to others to assess their own life project, was wholly selfless.

Guido's colleagues often turned to him for solutions to problems they couldn't solve. He gave them everything he had, including his kindness, affection and unconditional generosity. He became a protagonist in others' lives, but didn't want to be seen. Silent and humble, strong and comforting, Guido brought precious value to whatever he gave his attention to. He was a mentor behind the scenes, enriching others with his quiet presence.

Guido was a good listener; people heard him through his intense presence. He conversed with his silence, and a few well-chosen words. He conveyed his joy through his great irony. Everyone was in awe of his authority.

This is the real innate power of us human beings—it is love that truly makes us realize how valuable we are. In that sense, Guido is the perfect example of how one can put one's life at the service of others, for their good, with respect and love.

When people called me crazy, Guido was quick to point out, "Those who are crazy don't become crazy". His words reached my innermost core. I was seen as crazy because I could transcend reality; but those who couldn't do that, are actually themselves crazy.

When we decided to live together, Guido immediately found the wonderful place, Babuccio, which eventually became a den of art and culture. It became a hub for the Roman intelligentsia such as Michelangelo Antonioni, Eugenio Battisti, Carmelo Bene, Ruggero Orlando, Manfredo Tafuri, David and Dory Zard.

Guido spoiled everyone, just as he spoiled me. He was a gracious host and a great cook who thoroughly enjoyed feeding many people. Paul Stephen, the well-known American television choreographer and a close friend who lived in the lane nearby, once said, "Patrizia is a perfect husband and Guido, a perfect wife!"

For me, Guido was a father, mother, son, daughter, brother, sister, lover, husband, wife, manager, sponsor, administrator, bureaucrat, lawyer, adviser, poet, genius. I too was everything to him. I gave him all that I was able to give as he had done with me. He spoilt me, left me to create and do nothing else. I was always all over the world, but I came back to him who was always waiting for me, ever faithful. I could feel his protective arms around me even from far away. I could have renounced everything for him, but not my freedom.

Guido suffered up to his death. Everybody is the author of his own life, he chose me in spite of my need for complete freedom; I could have loved him only by being totally free. At that time, I couldn't do otherwise. Until we address the underlying causes, the same dynamics continue to surface. Guido was a truly unique human being—not just for me!

Guido's father, Alberto Menocci, was an engineer from Tuscany. He was sent to Tripoli for the reconstruction of the city. He was tall, sophisticated like Guido, and shared my passion for Indian culture. At our first meeting, he gave me books on India from his library.

Guido's kind and poetic mother dedicated her life to bringing up Guido and his sister Luisa. When I first met her after one of my shows, she was thrilled that her son was with me. Guido's face would light up each time he shared his memories about the years he spent in the countryside of Tuscany.

Guido was born in a shelter under constant threat of bombings in wartime Tripoli. I always believed that perhaps he developed a sense of guilt towards his mother who had given him life in such stressful conditions since he had experienced the first breath and had the first glimpse of the world amidst terror, which would mark his existence. I felt that he wanted to be sucked back into her womb for protection. On the one hand, he did everything to support others even at the cost of himself, but on the other, sought refuge in me the mother-woman, just as I saw in him, the father whom I could trust, but in reality, without being able to do so.

Guido accepted my strong boundaries but never urged me to break them down, thus keeping me united with him always. We were artists who turned to our art as an escape from ourselves. I simply danced, abandoning my life as a woman. He stopped courting me as a woman and gave everything to me as an artist. What a mistake on the part of both of us!

We were both too young not to make mistakes. The relationship between us could have been described as abnormal, crazy, neurotic but from the very beginning it went much beyond, thanks to him, not to me. In the end it went even further, thanks to me, not him.

I remember a dream, the first I had about him. I was twenty-eight years old and travelling to Orissa amidst temples and the countryside. Then I chanced upon a fairy tale oasis of crystal blue water surrounded by emerald green plants.

Guido who was looking sadly at me, collapsed on his knees. Then I found myself at his bedside, with love and inner strength. This is what unfortunately transpired prior to the terminal phase of his illness—first in the hospital, then in the hospice.

Around forty years later, one evening he collapsed on his knees and, I stayed by his side for months, nursing him without a moment's pause, with the same love and strength as I saw in my dream. It is incredible how the soul transcends time and space as we sleep and predict what will occur in the distant future.

We got married on 5 April 2014 at the Spallanzani Hospice. I remained beside him until the end just like I have always been close to him in the forty years of our sharing everything, even when I was far away in India or New York. My husband kept his happy look of the *puer*, of wonder, looking far into the distance ...

On 21 April 2014, Guido, my greatest and only friend, left me alone. A true friend is one who is ready to give his life for you, but above all, he should be ready to live for you. To share joy is to multiply it; to share sorrow is to dissipate it.

The final days made of serenity and subtle understanding between us were intense and sublime. Guido was ecstatic in the face of death; I was too. We were there for each other no matter what and we shared a deep, intimate joy. Guido did not know that he was dying when I married him, and I decided not to tell him. How could I have told him that the internal bleeding could start at any moment? Instead I preferred to celebrate life. At that point, what was the need for truth? Ever a champion of truth at any cost, I chose the surreal. I was close to him with all my love and nothing else, a love made of silence and intensity just like the last moments of a life spent together.

How lovely Guido had looked in his original thinness and he was even more lovely now, his face changed by the last breath, making him look relaxed and serene almost like Christ. He has been my angel, though in appearance he was more like the Biblical Moses. Everything he liked, I liked, and vice versa. We spent a lifetime devoted to one another despite being at long distance most of the times. Distance is good for love.

Just like Papa betrayed Mamma with a blonde, Guido betrayed me with illness. He abandoned me by dying. He was beaten by that cruel illness that kills about half of the humankind.

When life gets hard, we tend to get sick in our body and mind. The hardest thing to achieve is lightness. Life is a journey full of difficult challenges that inspire us to become better. Guido had a marvellous life. It was a significant irreparable loss, an unbridgeable loss.

A few months after he left me forever, I wrote to him:

Guido

chissà se voi lassù non godete delle sensazioni che la bellezza e la grandezza della natura suscita in noi nel suo immenso mistero

voi vivete direttamente nel mistero

ma il bello della vita qui in terra è ciò che ho appena compreso ed è questo che fa la differenza tra noi qui e voi là noi qui tra la gioia e il dolore voi là oltre entrambi dove si sta meglio

peggio in che consiste la differenza Guido dimmelo tu in sogno per favore dimmi come stai spiegamelo tu la vita è giocata tutta tra il partecipare e il fingere di farlo per una misteriosa paura di abbandonarsi nel farlo questa è la differenza

Guido so che ancora oggi tutto il meglio di te agirà in me e tutto il meglio di me agirà in te stanno già agendo.

Guido
I wonder if up there you
enjoy the sensations
that the beauty and grandeur
of nature arouse in us
in its immense mystery
you dwell in mystery
yet the beauty of life here on earth
is what I've just grasped
and this is what makes the difference between us
here me and you there
us here between joy and pain
you over there beyond both
where is better worse
what makes the difference
Guido speak to me in a dream
please tell me how you are
you explain it to me
life is played either with full participation or merely pretending
to do so
for a mysterious fear
of suffering in doing so
this is the difference
Guido I know that even now
the best of you will act in me
and the best of me will act in you

That night, Guido came in my dream, as an answer to my verses. When I brought an item he had made to a noblewoman, she informed me that it was damaged. Smiling and serene, Guido took it in his hand, closed it and opened it to reveal a man's shoe, ancient and precious with gold inlays and embedded gems.

My interpretation of the dream is that Guido wasn't understood by the world for his genius, here expressed by the misunderstanding of the noblewoman, and the shoe represented our precious path of love, made of tangible objects, to become eternal and "jewelled with joy". I am able to integrate Guido's values which are resonating within me now.

I believe that friendship is of the utmost value among all human relationships; in fact, it should be the *conditio sine qua non* of any relationship.

On reading the poem, Claudio Strinati, eminent art historian, critic and curator, said to me, "I have rarely had the chance to experience such a true, sincere and profound testimony as this one you sent me, but do you realize that you are talking about yourself?"

"You have rightly understood that I was also speaking of myself because one can easily understand something only after experiencing it personally. I understood Guido and his values now because I have the same values within myself. In this sense, yes, I also spoke about myself. You understand fully that which you have been observing and studying only when you experience it yourself. But it will resonate with you only if you already have those unrecognized qualities within you, which are your personal legacy," I replied.

We truly understand art only when we are able to enter its dynamism which is already our own. That is why it is difficult for geniuses to be understood.

I felt I had lost everything when I had lost Guido. At the time, a friend told me, "After having directed a dance company for forty years, that too in Italy, you can do anything in life." This was a great encouragement because I was mourning, and dancing did not come naturally to me.

It was as easy for me to go back to dancing as it is for a fish to swim when thrown back into the water after being left out for a while, but when I had to face the practical aspects of life without Guido, I was scared. I felt like a fish forced to fly or a bird forced to swim.

After losing Guido, I ventured into a truly impossible feat for someone like me. My father used to say to me: "You think of one thing and then go and do a thousand other things".

It has always been like this for me. I am like the element mercury that cannot remain still. In keeping with my nature of always being on the move, I began to transform Babuccio, the apartment which I had shared with Guido and which had also served as our studio, into a guest house with a special ambience.

"Every time I see you, you manage to amaze me, even though I already knew that it will happen because with you it's inevitable!" exclaimed Claudio Strinati when he saw the guest house, adding, "He who doesn't expect the unexpected won't discover truth," quoting Heraclitus.

Renovating Babuccio was a project that Guido had been working on for a long time, optimizing the spaces in a brilliant way. Unfortunately, I had to do it without him. Babuccio, a stone's throw from the exquisite Trevi Fountain, which is located in a small square, with houses behind it, which made that huge pool become the square itself.

In the 1980s, I had a really vivid dream in which an enormous eagle was circling above the fountain, almost touching the houses. Later in a psychoanalytic session, we deduced that the eagle was a symbol of the masculine-paternal. Guido was the powerful eagle that flew high, and harmoniously in a circle, which means completeness. Guido was whole.

After a year of mourning, in which I had lived benumbed with grief, I found, thanks to Guido, the fortitude to act. I created our guest house all by myself. The artist, spoiled by the architect who had always kept all problems far from her, now ventured into such an undertaking! Frightened of everything, fearful of being overwhelmed by everyone, I was about to start the renovation work at Babuccio when my mother passed away.

As I write this, I distinctly remember her saying, "A woman should always have a man next to her, if only symbolically, to be respected in society." I firmly dismissed that idea. That regressive perception of femininity did not sit well with me; I demonstrated firmness, toughness, determination and aggression. It was tiring and difficult, but I succeeded. With great satisfaction I felt reassured that I could face any of life's travails on my own.

I find that I possess the creativity that Guido instilled in me in all aspects of my everyday existence. I am still slowly discovering it in myself. And he imbibed from me the commitment and the courage of an artist to focus with all his energy on his own art. I know for sure he is realizing those qualities in the beyond and developing them in order to return to earth to accomplish something even more important than what he had already done. He had already shown what a great human being he had been.

When Guido left me, I thought I would not continue the dance company. This was my way of staying faithful to him. The company was ours and without him I did not want to continue it.

My purpose in life is to create the same connection in human relationships that I create one with my art.

To commemorate the fortieth year of our company, one of my collaborators, Claudio Di Gioia, invited me to write this book. I agreed because I felt compelled to leave behind my testimonial of what I had experienced and understood in my life. A legacy for everyone to read, especially for those I have loved, even when it did not seem so.

4

The "Queen" Escapes from the Clutches of the "King"

A few days ago, I saw two very young twin girls who struck me as extremely beautiful. Both were eating fruits. One of them was chewing the fruit with great relish, concentrating exclusively on the purely physical pleasure of eating while the other girl, smiled brightly conveying vitality and the joy of living. She was clearly focused on the inner delight she was experiencing.

That, I think, is the difference between love and power, and joy and superficial pleasure. Those who prioritize physical pleasure over spiritual pleasure should value those who impart the latter. Because the latter add great value to their existence, even if only with their presence. They have a powerful energy that can awaken others' souls. Everyone smiles, but only a few set off a light that spreads beyond themselves to the other.

At that moment, it occurred to me that the mother should have made sure to encourage both children to value each other and take inspiration from each other. To ensure that the second child learned to appreciate the concreteness and the ability of her sister to manage reality and the first one to perceive her sister's creative and spiritual energy. Otherwise these attributes could become a source of rivalry rather than a means for using their individual strengths to benefit each other.

The primary issue is spiritual in nature, which is why it is so fundamental.

What is inner joy?

I am convinced that this joy in which one experiences serenity and confidence generates courage, but not that of a fighter. It is the courage to surrender.

This is what I feel when I dance. Joy emanates from the strength to which we are always connected, except when we imagine we have lost it because of our insecurities, anxieties and fears. Mindlessly chasing worldly pleasures can also be distracting and rob us of our inner joy. Actually we have not lost it; we simply do not perceive it anymore because we are distracted. Joy always shines from within us.

In this regard, I have an anecdote to share from my childhood. My dearest friend Luciana and I studied dance together from the age of six. Luciana was a true artist. Olivia, her sister, was the most difficult person in her life; the one who created the deepest of difficulties and fragilities, forcing her to confront her limits and her weaknesses. Only one's real enemies know how to do this.

Their mother named Olivia in honour of her greatest love, her fiancé Oliver who was killed by the defeated fascists at the end of the war in an act of revenge. Oliver was an engineer and so was Olivia. I believe that their mother projected on Olivia her unconscious desire to fill the void left by this loss.

In my experience as an emotional freedom techniques (EFT) practitioner I have learned that relationships between siblings are the most difficult to manage and work out. Parents serve as role models whereas brothers and sisters being on the same side of the hierarchical demarcation line, stand side by side. Any comparison between them takes place on a level playing field, for good or bad, in harmony and admiration or in rivalry and competition.

According to the law of karma, often known as the law of cause and effect, we choose our parents and the birth environment. The essence of our existence lies in our relationship with our parents. This is what we need to strengthen ourselves, to reinforce our unexpressed potential and to overcome our limitations with which we come into this world.

I became convinced that the bond between siblings are karmically related to the root of how they will relate to others. The reactions that emerge from the dynamics of sibling connection correlate to the reactions that they will have in all human interactions. They hold an excellent mirror in which we can see ourselves and grow by working on our own issues which, if not addressed, will recur in all human interactions in the future. A child without siblings will have other kinds of challenges that I would prefer not to discuss here.

If the greatness of the ego is proportional to the intensity of fear, and fragility is proportional to both, then my dear friend Luciana was born with immense fragility and sensitivity. Sometimes, parents can make glaring mistakes, and in this case, Luciana's mother instilled severe mistrust in both sisters.

Olivia was a year and a half when Luciana was born. The new baby unwittingly took away all the attention from her immediately. Olivia had been born after a very difficult labour. The umbilical cord had almost strangulated her, leaving her with a black and blue face. It must have been difficult for her mother to hide her true feelings. I always imagined and understood that Olivia must have suffered from her mother's instinctive rejection. On the other hand, the mother had fallen in love with the beautiful Luciana from the moment she laid eyes on her.

I was told this and later was a witness to it. I saw Luciana's mother reveal this unconscious reaction to the end of her days. Her face would light up on seeing Luciana and darken when she saw Olivia. She did love and admire Olivia's strong personality, her practical nature, intelligence and goodness but the instinctive love she felt for Luciana was missing in her relationship with Olivia.

Luciana's mother passed on to her the creative side and to Olivia her practical side, thus unintentionally creating a rift between them. Being unable to reconcile the integration of the two opposite parts in herself, she gave each of her daughters one part of herself. Through Luciana she realized her aspirations to be an artist, and through Olivia, the concrete, realistic aspects of life. Of course she was not even aware that she had a bias towards Luciana and made every effort to treat both her daughters equally, constantly emphasizing how they were loved in the same way, even dressing them like twins to show that she was not being unfair.

When Luciana was a little girl, she told me in confidence that she did not want to become a mother until she had resolved her inner demons, conflicts and fears created by her familial situation.

A mother, like a true master, should guide her children to strengthen their weak points, which I like to call "weak muscles", rather than encouraging only those aspects in which they are already strong. That is what the girls' mother should have done with them; instilled practical skills in Luciana and helped her sister realize that not everyone is born with artistic talent, but she can appreciate it in others.

It is not easy to realize this. To realize means to accept the law of karma, which states that everyone is the author of their own life, is responsible for it and gets what they deserve.

Initially Luciana instinctively sympathized with Olivia, but she was digging a grave, which she was not aware of as she would later be, thanks to the Jungian psychoanalytic path she followed. Luciana would become aware that she had been a victim of hidden oppression and perversion disguised as good intent.

Since she was the elder sister, Olivia exercised her power because she was unable to feel love for her sister. How could she? Her mother had not made her experience love by making her feel her own.

We give others only what we know how to give to ourselves, just like on a flight, we are told to put on our oxygen mask first and then help others with theirs.

As Luciana grew older, her initial reaction to her sister's overwhelmingly domineering manner turned into an exaggerated and extreme rebelliousness and provocative behaviour in herself. Even today, when I see this type of relationship between siblings, my sympathy goes in favour of those who reflect Olivia rather than those who represent Luciana, the so-called spoilt mama's child.

She rebelled deep inside against being raised like that but she did not have the tools to manage what was happening. As an adult, Luciana would rebel. With all that rage built over the years, she provoked her sister to the point where she began to bite Olivia, and Olivia tried to rob her of her belongings.

Olivia's extreme greed was the consequence of the maternal message that had limited her to finding her personal value solely in the concreteness of material goods. Luciana reacted in the exact opposite way by cultivating a total disregard for material things and pursuing spiritual ones, until later when she rolled up her sleeves to build a healthy relationship with the material world in all its manifestations, especially sex, money, health and success. I witnessed Luciana's tremendous effort to achieve this goal.

Sex and money, despite their different dimensions, share a common root: they promise earthly pleasures. Money becomes a symbol of recognition of our own worth.

If we have an unresolved relationship with money, either too much attachment or disinterest in it and if we fail to have sufficient earnings, it is good to view these as the projection of our low self-esteem, and how we value ourselves. When we tell ourselves that money is not the highest priority, that there are other aspects of life that are more important or that money is not everything, we are disguising reality. The truth is that we do not value ourselves enough, we believe we do not deserve the money.

If we are free and fulfilled in one of the two dimensions—sex and money—we are proportionately equal in the other. Sex and money could be used as mirrors to understand where we are in our relationship with ourselves. I am convinced that greedy people have a perverted sexuality whereas those who are not interested in money are more sensual than sexual.

Sex and money awaken some sense of guilt in us. At the heart of every self-destructive reaction is a failure to recognize our worth because it has been stifled by the "fear" of succumbing, of not being able to reconnect with the original love within us. We can say that we are envious because we cannot see *within* ourselves and therefore we do not recognize our own value.

When we resolve the blocks generated by the instinctual reactions to external events in our childhood that have made us feel incapable, insecure and unworthy of respect and love, everything changes as if by magic, and we begin to attract money. Like everything else we no longer project our problems, but only our resolutions.

Those who prioritize material pursuits derive a physical pleasure from them and deprive themselves of the spiritual joy that comes with love and art. I can't imagine how they feel, save for moments of physical and psychological pleasure at feeling powerful. I don't think they are all right.

Two wings are required to fly. Their mother did not realize that by encouraging her daughters to fly with only one wing she was cutting off the other. Luciana's impulse to rebel against all that is unhealthy and unjust made her a fighter rather than a depressed person. Today, she knows very well that it is true compassion for the pain of the wicked that can improve things to some extent. Evil is overcome by actively moving towards good, rather than fighting it. Luciana learned this lesson "on her skin", that is very intensely.

Olivia was given the responsibility of taking care of the little one. But she continued to project on Luciana the sense of maternal rejection she suffered—amplified and aggravated by the profound pain that followed.

She channelled the rancour she felt against her mother on her sister who was the most vulnerable.

Luciana once told me that during recess in elementary school that Olivia did not want her on her team because she thought Luciana was clumsy and would make her team lose. Obviously she was taking revenge for what she believed she had taken away from her.

This dynamic triggers a tumult of conflicts and bipolarity between love and hate.

Olivia was regularly distressed before oral tests because she couldn't bear the thought of not being able to prove herself the best. Luciana faced school challenges lightly and was content to do well without feeling the need to excel because what she was really interested in was dance. Like me.

Luciana, like me, relied heavily on her ability to recall what she had learned in class and improvise on the subject. We took the evening classes on dance at the Academy and also studied English together. So there was very little time and energy left to prepare for the oral tests in the morning. Luciana's life like mine, demanded twice the effort, and she needed a way to survive. In the night, she would replicate the homework that her friends dictated to her over the phone.

Olivia had long, thick, red hair; the hairdressers said they had never seen so much hair, enough for three heads. I believe this is also true of her intelligence. She was a water diviner who could tell where underground water was to be found, by using a stick. I always felt the strength of her esoteric nature. Like Luciana, she knew how to grasp people's unconscious truths.

But a continuous slew of disparaging experiences, even the smallest, made Luciana close herself, sink into a black hole and cultivate a sense of guilt for being the cause of so much pain. Gradually, a deep sorrow began to grow in her and a distrust of the other's inability to understand and accept her value as different, for not taking her as she was, but as abnormal.

"Not abnormal," Dr Carosi, an anthroposophical doctor, would tell her later at their first meeting. "Out of the norm", he said to help Luciana understand who she was, what her true nature was and her special value.

Luciana paid for the mistakes of her mother who deprived her of the possibility of having a sister like Olivia as a friend. But Olivia refused to accept her responsibilities to her sister, nor did she ever deal with the problems she had developed as a result of her hatred.

I must say that as Luciana's best enemy, she was strong and intense and therefore it was worth it for Luciana. She continued to attract people who triggered these reactions, but for her these harsh adversaries pale in comparison to the power of her sister Olivia, with whom she has been able to strengthen herself to the point where they cannot even scratch her. People of this nature cannot bear to witness the success of others; they describe it in terms of denigration, a projection of the unconscious self-denigration because they will never be able to do what they see others doing. It is always sad to have to deal with their unhealthy thoughts and actions.

Those who have been forced to choose power and cannot get out of the self-destructive spiral of this choice, lack the humility to question themselves, which is why they cannot reawaken their will to do it. To survive, they must demonize people like Luciana, who with superhuman effort, succeed in being reborn from the ashes in which these mechanisms had buried her. Behind this attitude the subtle affirmation of their own power is always hidden.

Luciana learned to detect the subtle nuances of power from her sister. Furthermore, Luciana also intensely suffered the emotion of oppression and worked hard to analyze and understand it. Luciana is a well-known musician. She internalized the essence of this experience in such a deep way that it became a theme for her art and it was projected very dramatically in her earlier compositions. However, her music became more spiritual and poetic later on.

Luciana and I have much in common, especially irony which emerged from her experiences with her sister. Either you develop irony or you die. Irony is really the subtext of humour.

I have a compelling anecdote to share about my relationship with power. I will not name the politician involved. Not out of for fear of retaliation, but out of good etiquette.

I was with the gallerist Giancarlo Iosimi at a Premio Strega event when the particular politician passed us with his retinue. He stopped to greet us, showed interest in getting to know me and gave me his business card. I called on him as he had requested, since he was then in charge of the Ministry of Culture from which I had been receiving funding for years, for the activities of my modern dance company Patrizia Cerroni & I Danzatori Scalzi.

He received me in an office that I would call a palace, with an enormous room where, in addition to me, he had marshalled half of Italy—superintendents, art directors and well-known journalists, in a continuous flow of people. My first impression was that I was in the court of the Sun King. He was extremely clever, funny, possessing inexhaustible knowledge. The "king" invited me to sit beside him, just like a queen, and began introducing me to the courtiers, but never giving me the chance to talk.

After a few hours, I began to get restless and hinted that I wanted to leave. Immediately two dandies, tall, thin and suave, one French (with a bow tie) director of the Gallery of Modern Art and the other English (without bow tie) approached and told me, in a gentle but strange manner, that I could not leave.

I felt like a sacrificial victim.

Okay, let's see where this is going, I told myself.

I gave them the impression that I was accepting the passive role of an ornament. Fortunately, some of my friends arrived—the journalist Marco Dolcetta, who had conducted a well-publicized interview with

Craxi in Tunisia and Superintendent Gianni Bullian, at whose invitation I had performed *Ali in Corpo (Wings in the Body)* at Castle of L'Aquila. I began to feel at ease and even more so with the arrival of Rita Paris, director of the villa of the Quintili, who ignoring the king embraced me with enthusiasm.

Without missing a beat, he gave the command, "Let's all go to the Quintili!" And so we did.

A caravan of cars with dozens of people, including the dandies left for the villa. We also had a well-known journalist who took notes by hanging on the lips of the king.

Bah, what a strange situation! Let's see how it ends, I thought.

As we walked around the Villa dei Quintili, Rita was laughing and joking about our childhood in Ursulines convent. When she began to talk enthusiastically about my show *Ma volete capire qualcosa di noi donne??!!* (But do you really want to understand something of us women??!!), which she had seen in Rome a few months before, the king became annoyed by the recognition of my artistic value.

I understood my role for the day. From that moment, I began to challenge him silently.

The king gave another command, "And now all shall proceed for dinner!"

The caravan moved slowly and stopped at a restaurant near the Chamber of Deputies. The owner of the restaurant had offered us dinner. I was again forced to sit next to the king, with Setsuko the Japanese widow of the Polish-French modern artist Balthus on the other side. After finishing dinner, he issued a new diktat, "And now all to my house!"

The magic circle tightened as we were about thirty at his home. My antennas were on high alert. Being curious and adventurous, I enjoy challenges and playing with danger is my metier.

The king invited me on a tour of his house, a well-known strategy to make beautiful girls fall into the net. I accepted, and tried to appear calm, as he took my hand and moved forward. I didn't turn to look at the expression of the dandies because I could imagine it.

They don't know who they are dealing with! I'm an athlete and there are thirty people in the house! *I can easily have the situation under control. I know how to accelerate on a curve, in the worst-case scenario,* I thought.

I was lost in my thoughts, when I suddenly realized that we were standing in front of his bedroom; I halted with no intention of entering it. He sent me a quick sideways glance and clasped me in a horrible iron grip with his arms, which felt like a pair of ice-cold pincers, hurting me.

I don't know how but I broke away, sliding out like an eel, and sprinted to catch up with the others. It was then that I realized what it could mean to suffer sexual violence. The aggressor had no erotic impulses, only an evil, malicious intent of hurting the other to subdue her. For some people, this is the only way to experience pleasure.

The dandies, seeing me return so prematurely, gave me stern looks. I imagined them with hands on their hips to emphasize the reproach, their thin lips compressed in a grimace. I was equally certain that they too visualized me in the famous gesture *il gesto del vaffa* (the Italian elbow fuck).

I spent the whole day without the opportunity to talk about my projects even for a moment! That was the whole purpose of my going to that meeting.

With all the difficulties, impediments and barriers that many artists encounter on their journey, this is how those who support art and culture, play their cards. The power they wield should be experienced as a mission, but this is how they fulfil their duties. Here's what he who has the power does with it.

After a good quarter of an hour, he arrived and sat alone on a sofa. I joined him to tell him with a naive, sweet and tender expression, and blinking my eyes, "You should not have done that, you scared me!"

Lounging on the sofa with fingers locked behind his head, he replied happily, "You see, until now you've only had fags!"

I swear, these were his exact words. But in my opinion it was an unconscious confession—*he was talking about himself.*

And with that I left for home.

The next day, we were all supposed to leave on his private plane for Venice for the Balthus exhibition. I wouldn't have gone there even if he had multiplied my funding a hundredfold! I phoned him to tell him I would not go to Venice with him. He reacted with "Careful, the erotic burst doesn't last long."

"There was nothing erotic; that was just an impulse of sexual possession, an attempt to abuse your power. Please do not confuse the sacred with the profane!"

Thanks to that experience, I finally understood how the world works. It turned out to be a valuable experience for it helped me understand the dynamics of power. I finally knew how to react instead of being a victim. I must add though that he did not cancel the funding I had previously enjoyed.

I saw him at his house the day he was interviewed by Rai after the stir that he had caused on a visit to Berlin. As soon as he saw me, he immediately noticed that I had changed my hair style and colour! Always alert and attentive.

I had called him that day because I had dreamed that we were together on an enjoyable trip to Australia, holding hands happily and peacefully. I was not afraid of him anymore. I had already handled his abuse head-on, so I knew he would never try that again.

He actually left for Australia the next day. Ah, my dreams also inform me of secret facts.

I have always reacted to blackmail and abuse with irony and sarcasm.

Love or power: if one is lacking, we cultivate the other. It is rare and difficult to realize the power of love, but it is easy to cultivate the love of power.

My life has never been regulated by power games, but by games of love. There is no fear when you love. May the heavens grant that all persons in positions of authority follow in the footsteps of those who choose to love themselves through daily effort and draw strength from the source of love buried under the rubble. May the heavens reawaken in them the will to do so. Instead of demonizing and envying those who refuse their impositions, may the heavens make them accept the example of those who do so.

The good sublimates the body, the evil incarnates the soul.

5

On the Road in the Seventies

We go back to the 70s now.

My great French master Jean Cebron and I forged a deep friendship after I graduated from the Academy. Using his original choreography based on silence, *Mobile*, interpreted by Beatrice Libonati, who subsequently joined the Pina Bausch company in Essen, he took part in the inaugural performance of I Danzatori Scalzi (The Barefoot Dancers). He frequently spent evenings at my place while he was in Rome for extended periods. We enjoyed drinking—sometimes a lot—late into the night, and Guido the perfect host that he was, let us do that. Jean the Parisian, often cooked us an excellent roast beef, but it was too buttery for me. I was always on a diet.

On one such night, at three o'clock, Jean decided to go home, that too on a scooter, after having drunk too much. I tried to persuade him in every possible way to sleep at our place, but he simply did not want to listen to reason. I was wrong not to force him to stay. I should have prevented him from going out by placing myself adamantly in front of the door. But I didn't. I was too young. Today, I certainly would not allow anyone to leave in that state and definitely not on a scooter.

That night Jean met with an accident and fractured his skull. They called me from the hospital at dawn. He was in a coma and it seemed that he would not make it. But he made it! Guido and I hosted him for several months at Babuccio and had him treated. He needed great assistance at that time and in that state. He came out stronger after that incident.

I frequently travelled to Germany on tour. Luckily Jean attended all my performances there since he was teaching in Germany at that time, thus he continued to be my mentor with his insightful, helpful and affectionate remarks. We lost touch with one another after he returned to teach permanently at the Essen school.

He had retired to the north of France and although he was over ninety he would often call me and cheerfully chat with me in his childlike voice, talking in a mixture of Italian, French and English. He was always almost incomprehensible, but words never mattered in our relationship. He left us on 1 February 2019.

In the early 1970s, the company Teatrodanza Contemporanea di Roma (Contemporary Dance Theater of Rome) was founded by five American and four Italian choreographers: Bob Curtis, Marcia Plevin, José De Vega, Joseph Fontano, Jacqueline Puglisi, Nicoletta Giavotto, Gianfranco Paoluzzi, Elsa Piperno and me.

Teatrodanza was born from the idea of creating a company that would allow each one of us to showcase our distinct style of choreography. Then each one of us would dance to the other's choreography. We called the company Teatrodanza Contemporanea di Roma because at the time it was crucial to spread awareness that dance is also theatre. Also, the only forms of dance available in Italy were classical ballet in opera houses and modern dance on television for those who wanted to dance professionally. We were the first to offer something different.

Elsa Piperno and Bob Curtis financed the first show. We practised at a dance school with spacious, light-filled rooms on Via dell'Orso, close to the city square Piazza Navona. Here Bob taught "primitive" dance, an African dance style, while Elsa taught the Graham technique of modern American dance pioneered by Martha Graham.

I had previously produced three pieces at the Academy that demonstrated my potential as the future of Italian dance, with a fully formed language of my own. I completed my fourth piece of choreography with Teatrodanza, a solo for José De Vega, who played one of the major characters Chino in the groundbreaking musical *West Side Story*.

It was a significant event because following the solo dance, I participated for the first time as a choreographer for a group performance of *Aiko Baye* to Ginger Baker's music.

We made our debut at the historic Parioli Costanzo Theatre in Rome. The pettiness, the competitiveness, the abuse and the power games within the company, compelled me to leave it. The final drop that made the water overflow from the vase was this: Jose and I had performed a *pas de deux* at the Academy of Dramatic Art in Rome, and after the demonstration show during the day, we were getting the usual enthusiastic applause in the courtyard when a film director came up to us.

He told us that he had already spoken to the show's promoter that we were the perfect pair to play the role of Adam and Eve in his next film. We were willing to discuss it with him, although we both felt that we would not really be interested in the part, as it sounded quite kitschy.

Unaware that the director had already spoken to us, the promoter revealed at a company meeting the following day that she and José had been selected for a film. She thought she was sharing the good news with him for the first time. I never imagined that José could get so angry. He got up and, with fiery red eyes, refuted her story, telling everyone what had actually happened, that the director wanted me with him, not her. Since it was she who presented the show to the public, the director had asked for her permission to have us in the film. She presumably believed she could convince the director to take her in place of me by telling him I had other commitments.

Jose and I protested against this vile attempt at manipulation and walked out of the meeting, slamming the door behind us. I had been with the company for two years. For me, it was an act of courage because I could see only a desert on the horizon wherein I could develop my choreographies. Life rewards the audacity of those who are honest, and the choice I made brought me wonderful fruit.

Shortly afterwards, Marcia Plevin and Bob Curtis also left the company and created another group with me. We performed at the Spazio Zero theatre in Trastevere, which is often used for avant-garde theatrical performances. That association was the *trait-d'union* that led to the formation of my group, I Danzatori Scalzi (The Barefoot Dancers) shortly after I returned from New York.

I love New York, the Big Apple, the city where every type of excellence in the world is found. This is because it is a city that greatly values high quality in everything. It is work all the time, but with the same intensity with which children play.

Have you noticed that when children play they are super-focused and give their best? If it were not so, they would not have fun. Have you ever seen anyone play with laziness, sloppiness or carelessness? Of course not!

New Yorkers have great creativity in everyday life, just as those who are always playing. Astrologically, New York city falls under the sign of Cancer, the same as Guido, and it reminds me of all his qualities. Even though New York is huge, it has a warm welcoming vibe, but like all metropolises, it can be evil too.

Even India, which is under the sign of Pisces, has the element of water like Cancer, has an easy-going atmosphere. Naturally, there are challenges to overcome in order to maintain the creative flow; otherwise, it would be dull, but these issues are not insurmountable.

In both these places I feel supported in all of my endeavours because the creative energy prevails as the primary force behind everything.

To win on the everyday creative is the sensuous delight of living in comfort and beauty in Italy, the birthplace of the greatest geniuses in all fields—art, culture, science and sport—who are admired worldwide.

Seas, mountains, lakes, hot springs, the countryside, plenty of sunshine, the perfect climate, the best food in the world, and the highest quality of life are all found in the beauty and diversity of nature in Italy. You could spend the happiest time here!

Whereas in the workplace, it is more like trying to break through a wall of resistance. Nothing works smoothly: there is so much carelessness laxity, so many hitches and hindrances. In this, Rome is *caput mundi*. It is difficult to do anything here, especially dance.

Rome is my hometown and I tell you with pride, that it is a unique place known for its beauty and strength. It is a more esoteric and magical metropolis than any other in the world because of this unique blend. Magnificent, isn't it?

Like me Rome falls under the astrological sign of Leo, which is associated with the heart. Its motto is "I can". Like many Romans, Papa had a big heart and was far-sighted, but with a dash of cynicism and irony. The same spirit has allowed the Eternal City, so nicknamed by history, to dominate the world and invent the most advanced engineering systems that amaze us even today, for their functionality and efficiency.

Even though I appreciate this great culture, I never found Latin or its literature to be particularly appealing since I found it too concrete, rational and masculine for me. Instead I loved the Greek world, and enjoyed studying and translating Greek tragedies in high school. That made me dream and travel to the east, which to my mind is an introspective, passionate and irrational culture, in one word, "feminine".

As the headquarters of the three powers—political, administrative and ecclesiastical—Rome sadly, is also an arrogant city where the stench of corruption permeates the air. Even a bartender can make you a good or a bad cappuccino, depending on how you behave with him. I hate this attitude, and that is why I am in conflict with everything and everyone. I have never approved of the Roman way of focussing on "managing" relationships often at the cost of merit and quality. I reacted to this by making myself disagreeable in every way. It was my way of reaffirming the professionalism my Milanese mother taught me. In fact, Milan is the New York of Italy from this point of view.

New York has proved me right by confirming that one *must* stake everything on one's own abilities. New York is the true home of modern dance, its headquarters, so it was natural that I would go there. It was very exciting for me to witness different languages of movement being practised by different artists with great freedom. It was the early 70s and modern dance was flourishing there. It was Marcia Plevin who introduced me to her friends who were happy to host me.

To my immense delight, I relocated many times in the six months of my stay in New York! I was thus able to get to know Manhattan and many of its neighbourhoods and each of which was a whole new world for me to discover. I am easy to host because I have always been very flexible and am content with little, even though I do enjoy the luxury of the seven-star hotels I am often put up in.

Consider that in Delhi I lived for four months in a *barsati*—a small apartment—on the top floor in Defence Colony hosted by my Indian friend Irpinder Puri, who was an actress at the time. I would sleep on a mattress on the floor of the veranda, bathe with buckets of water, which I like to do even today. I trained every day at two in the afternoon on the large terrace, under the blazing sun at 40 degrees Celsius because I enjoyed its warmth on my body.

On winter evenings we would make a fire and invite friends to dinner under the stars. Being a *stakanovista*, or a workaholic, I think that travelling with this mindset has strengthened my bones and made me an adventurous woman.

When I studied in Martha Graham's Dance Company in New York, she was already old and was no longer teaching. Since I was friends with some of her dancers, they made an exception and gave me a free place to stay at a company retreat in Washington. As a nineteen-year-old, I was welcomed and loved by all of them for my enthusiasm and because I contributed something special through my dancing and expressiveness. It was an unforgettable experience, of which I treasure beautiful memories, more human than artistic. I was not used to having my ideas and proposals acknowledged in Italy. In New York, I found openness and collaboration, support and friendship. A lot of Mexican marijuana was part of the package!

I even had a crush on one of the dancers, a classic blond, handsome and kind American athlete. He took me out for a boat ride on a lake. I experienced intense feelings of love and tenderness while under the hallucinatory influence of "Mexican", as though something that had been concealed deep inside me surfaced and was unveiled for the first time. It was very poetic and revealed the essence of what happens to me when I fall in love. It is the same experience when I dance and my audience shares the ecstasy but without the need for hallucinogens. Indeed, for me dance was enough.

Frankly, I don't think Martha Graham deserved the recognition she got. Her dance was limited and based on few elements, such as contraction and release and spiral, of which I have found only a few useful, but they have left no mark. Therefore, I disagree with the inestimable and epochal worth that was assigned to her. She was a powerful woman who knew how to achieve fame by cultivating contacts. Very similar to that presenter-promoter at Teatrodanza. Let us face it, it works the same way everywhere in the world, not only in Rome.

I have always had great interactions with the New Yorkers. Along with the technical and professional rigour, they strongly communicate to me that all is possible and give me the willpower to keep going. They understand that I am passionate and that I carry a kind of sensuality and eroticism different from theirs, which is more pragmatic than mine.

There was an arthouse cinema theatre, deserted now because of the August heat and the fumes that emanated from the subway. They had a Buster Keaton festival there and I didn't miss a single film. I had made friends with a French student who studied film, and he accompanied me almost every night. For me, Keaton is one of the greatest dancers, actors, directors and poets of all time. He was a dramatically comic actor, of such intensity that he could literally make you die laughing. I remember that when I saw *The General* with Guido, in an arthouse cinema in Trastevere, at a certain point I had to leave the room, holding my belly because my loud, uncontrollable laughter was painful. Everything that comes from him comes from the root of suffering, just like everything that is truly intense. In my heart, Keaton goes hand in hand with Mingus, and I rejoice being between them.

I found Charles Mingus to be the greatest jazz musician of all time, erotic, desperate, true, detached, serene but unprejudiced. This is the order of the adjectives that comes to my mind when I think of him. Mingus had truly grasped the circularity of existence. I loved him the first time I listened to him. And when he winked at me from the stage, I thought, *Okay, we have known always known each other ….* We are here for one another, a part of something bigger, just as one feels in real love. We artists always need to live in the experience of the Absolute. That is how we realize the circularity of existence.

Even if Guido was the love of my life—my safe harbour—I would still let myself drift into soft platonic infatuations, something most of us artists do. We need this falling in love.

With another student, I would go to Central Park on Sunday mornings, to make some dollars, selling whole grain sandwiches, which we had made the night before. The idea was mine, since it was the era of macrobiotics. Every Sunday was a sell-out. We had a lot of fun, we met lots of people and new friendships were born.

In the 1970s, New York was notoriously dangerous. One night I made the decision to travel alone to Soho in order to get over the paranoia that the overall environment of terror had forced me into and to show myself that I could go anywhere in the world and nothing bad would ever happen to me. It was beyond the boundaries of high-risk areas. I have always felt I was under a powerful divine protection and that evening I was determined to experience it.

In those days, one could get killed for a few dollars in central Manhattan, even during daytime. As I was walking on the streets, it felt like a scene from a movie—a dark night with streets full of derelict humans, drug addicts and alcoholics slammed to the ground, dead drunk. I was walking, looking straight ahead, acting like nothing was wrong, while I could hear voices from all directions trying to get my attention. Despite the adrenaline rush, I returned home with my heart in my throat, but from then on I never looked over my shoulders, either in New York or anywhere else in the world.

Among the many friends of friends who had put me up, one was an odd woman who lived uptown. She was a tall and lanky blonde, cold, emotionally detached and out of touch with reality. As an intellectual and scholar who had written books on racial issues, she considered herself to be an expert on black culture, calling black men her brothers. I slept in the room with her beautiful five-year-old child, with whom I established an immediate rapport. With blue eyes, long blond hair and a round, intelligent face, she looked like a little woman though she was so vulnerable, in great need of love that she could not receive from such a mother. She was looking at me as a safety anchor and I was delighted to be one for her.

One day, her mother announced that she would take us to Harlem.

"How?" I asked. "Isn't it dangerous for whites to cross the border?"

"Of course not!" she said. "You are safe with me, as I am considered one of them. I have written books on them, they are my brothers."

I agreed but reluctantly. I was extremely curious by nature. I couldn't believe I could enter Harlem, which was totally out of bounds for us whites. Today it is one of the most sought-after neighbourhoods. When we reached there we found some people in the square taking part in some kind of a rally. As she tried to make her way through the crowd, I stood back with the girl clutching my hand. I squeezed it to reassure her. A big, menacing black man told her mother that we couldn't stay there. We could sense that the situation was deteriorating. I could see her gesticulating, and him getting visibly irritated. Three other men arrived on the scene with heavy steps, and she continued to cajole her brothers. *Is she nuts?* I thought to myself She finally retreated. By then, the child was terrified and so was I. Suddenly, the men began to chase us while cursing aloud; we sprinted, with the child grabbing my hand even tighter. We managed to jump onto a bus. The mother joined us shortly afterwards. After recovering my breath, I couldn't stop myself from confronting her, "Sister! You are really foolish to come to this place, and that too with the child!"

This was my first American stay, which lasted six months. Though I did flirt with the idea of settling in New York I chose to return to Italy because Guido was waiting. Besides, there is always something that brings me back to Rome. Roma is Roma. Roma when read backwards is *amore*, meaning love in Italian. I really can't cut the umbilical cord with this city. Beautiful, but truly beautiful!

Would you like to step back with me into the 1970s and take a look at theatre and avant-garde cinema of that time? After the 1968 students' revolution, which marked a worldwide escalation of social conflicts, there was an extraordinary ferment that touched everything, including art and culture. In my opinion, only Surrealism was vital, revolutionary and liberating. It ditched logic, unleashed the unconscious and smashed social norms …. Pure creative chaos. I think that it was one of the most exceptional periods for Italian culture and art. Today it seems that there is a split between these two elements, art and culture. Then, for us artists, everything that took place in more strictly cultural domains was instantly incorporated into our experience. Dance, cinema, theatre, all the arts were in a sort of debate with each other. We were open to discussions, confrontations, disagreements and curious about what was happening in the other fields. Today, everything seems shallow; everything seems to be tacked on rather than interpenetrated.

I was considered the Carmelo Bene of dance—transgressive, provocative and rebellious. I have moved from darkness to light with my art since India. A reckless Patrizia precedes India, and is followed by a spiritual one.

I was working on the choreography for the Banco del Mutuo Soccorso concert "Come in un' ultima cena" (As in a Last Supper) at the time. I sent two of my dancers, Laura Morante, now a celebrated actress and

Enrica Palmieri, current director of the National Dance Academy, to invite Carmelo Bene to Babuccio, which was a few metres from the opera house Teatro Quirino where he was performing. He accepted the invitation immediately and came to see me with, guess who? Michelangelo Antonioni! The brilliant Italian film director, screenwriter and editor. I was stunned. I have long admired Michelangelo Antonioni, whom I still consider one of the greatest poets of contemporary cinema.

At their insistence, I timidly showed them my dance videos that had been shot for the sole purpose of archiving the choreographies on Super8 and Akai with fixed cameras. At the time, these were our high-tech instruments. You can imagine how I felt when I showed those videos to the legend of international cinema. Michelangelo greatly appreciated the unusual dance and gently put me at ease, saying that I did not have to worry if the shooting did not enhance it, it was compelling anyway. What a dear and noble soul he was!

Michelangelo would then often come to see my shows. We also found ourselves in each other's company in India on 1989 New Year's eve, to our great joy. On that occasion he surprised me again with his subtle humour, although we were in a spiritual retreat. We were lying on the ground in meditation under the stars, and he was sitting. He spoke in just the right pitch but in a mocking tone: "You all look like corpses!"

I recall having dinner with Carmelo Bene, Ruggero Orlando and Gigi Proietti in a restaurant near the Pantheon. Carmelo and Ruggero were engaged in funny verbal duel in which they used the rhythm of Greek metre in Italian. Carmelo described Proietti as a "stage animal", who was born for the stage. Carmelo had personality, culture and sensitivity, but he hadn't been able to develop a real language, which comes from very different sources and certainly not from distorting his voice even with poetry and geniality.

For me, Daniel Day-Lewis is a great example of how a genuine actor can be transformed into a role. He truly understands the process of negating oneself in order to become the character one plays. Since he draws directly from the character's personality, he does not feel the need to pull from his own. All his interpretations are masterly, especially the one in *My Left Foot* where he is a young man confined to a wheelchair as he suffers from cerebral palsy. He uses his willpower to show his extraordinary talent by painting with his left foot, the only part of his body that he can control. Daniel powerfully and intensely conveys the strength of the soul, which is unaffected by barriers when it comes to *creating* from the heart. The film is a masterpiece because of his interpretation.

Some examples of the avant-garde theatre of those years that influenced my work style by encouraging me to incorporate the theatrical element into the choreographies were Carmelo Bene, the bravery of transgression but in the self-denial of oneself; Giuliano Vasilicò, the strength of bodily expressiveness; Meme Perlini, the sense of happening but without self-irony; and the great Dario Fo, satire against power, are just a few examples of the avant garde.

The performances by Tadeusz Kantor and Peter Brook have left a bigger impact on me. I met the latter in Delhi at a diplomatic dinner, when he was preparing his show on the Mahabharata. I had the privilege of speaking at length with him. And I learned that we shared a common view of theatrical direction—one that is based on emptiness and fullness, a space without borders and the "Indian" sense of the infinite. Kantor, a brilliant painter, set designer and theatre director from Poland, much closer to my roots in German expressionism, made me experience the drama of whipping irony and the grotesque.

During that time, I frequented the studios of Mario Schifano and Franco Angeli, artists of the Roman School, and friends of Guido. Instinctively, I didn't like the dark energy of death in them. My friendship with Mario got deeper much later, in 1996, when Radisha, painter and sculptor friend of mine stayed in Rome for a long time.

I met Radisha on my first trip to India, which I will delve into in a later chapter. We were both in Varanasi, also known as Benares, as house guests of Balbir Singh Katt, an internationally renowned sculptor, who had displayed huge works in many cities of India and the world. You probably know that Balbir suddenly disappeared in 2000, creating a huge international controversy with his dramatic disappearance. We never knew what happened. He left his home for a walk and never returned. He was teaching at Banaras Hindu University then.

One day, I remember returning to his house and as always, lurking behind the majestic trees to wait for the right moment to cross the park, and thus avoid being attacked by monkeys of all sizes, when I noticed his house help, who cooked and cleaned his home, sitting around a fire with three or four strange men. The maid was young, very beautiful and refined, the men all had pinched faces. I felt that they were hatching some plan where she would seduce Balbir who was naive and childlike, as we artists often are and then blackmail him.

Besides Radisha and me, the Japanese sculptor Yoshin Ogata was also a guest of Balbir's. Over the course of one month we developed our friendship as artists. I have fond memories of Yoshin. We went to the hill of Varanasi from where we could see the funeral pyres burning in the open cremation ground. This was the first time I saw bodies burning. It was an experience that affected us both deeply. To see the ephemerality of life in the burning of flesh and bones, and to witness the human body coming to such an end, made me think about my father's death. Even Yoshin, like me, remained silent all day.

When I returned to Rome, I thought of introducing Radisha to the art world of the city by taking him to the galleries of my friends. The director of one of the galleries informed us that she would be visiting Mario Schifano's workshop on Via delle Mantellate in Trastevere the next day. I asked if we could accompany her so Mario could meet Radisha. She explained that Mario had a very difficult temperament and did not want new people around, but after some insistence on my part, she yielded, asking us to absolutely not speak, let alone identify ourselves. She said that in order to avoid upsetting him, it was preferable to look anonymous.

As soon as we walked into the studio, Mario asked, "Who are you?"

He grabbed my hand and almost dragged me into the private area of the house, ignoring the other guests. We talked for hours, as he was curious to know everything about my dance. I gave him my business card with the logo in black and white. Being extremely good with technology, he instantly enlarged it to the size of a poster and painted amazing coloured sketches all around it. He gave it to me, but I forgot to take it when I left the house and it was never found again. Every time I went to see him he would give me photos, posters and paintings including his famous series on television. One of them also included an Andy Warhol.

The relationship between Mario and myself was terribly painful for me. I was deeply drawn to him because he was tender, sweet and poetical at one moment but the next moment he could turn into the exact opposite, morbidly split between the good and the evil, the angel and the devil. During our time together, I imbibed his desperation as a true artist, exacerbated by the use of hard drugs, and then experienced depression for days.

Once I went to visit him in the day time on my bike, in a villa that he had rented at the Sabaudia dunes for the summer. The Sabaudia is a place where the might and compassion of nature coexist, giving people who see it a sense of liberation and transformation. The sea water is always clear, and the air seems to oxygenate every cell. Next to it, the evergreen Circeo mountain is meek and at peace in its full surrender, to teach that this is the only possible condition in which to love by letting yourself be loved. I find the same characteristics in my feminine nature, of strength and kindness, and my thoughts are influenced by it.

I feel balanced and sure of myself; I seem to be able to overcome my limits, which become clearer because I observe them with the same detachment in which nature lets itself live.

On that day, Mario painted happily as we talked till late at night. At one point, for no apparent reason, he angrily threw my bike into his Mercedes and dumped me back home.

Fortunately, my sister-friend from New York, Joanne Roberts, who was then a well-known producer for CNN and my guest in Rome, came to rescue me from him and his depressive influences. By making the American gesture of index fingers meeting crosswise, as if to say *"Vade retro Satan"* (Get thee behind me Satan), she dissuaded me from starting any romantic relationship with him because she knew it would destroy me. However, her then boyfriend, Nick, who composed film music, did not think so. I listened to our female wisdom. I refused to let Mario Schifano ruin me. Now Joanne's house in New York is mine, my home in Rome is hers. With Radisha, it is the same with his home in Santa Fe, where he now lives.

After Mario's funeral in 1998 I cut out a picture of him as a young man from a newspaper article. I did not notice right away that on the sheet behind that image, there was a photo of Bacon's hideous mask, the same size and exact replica of Mario's photograph. What a strange and incredible coincidence! He, his duplicate, the splitting of the I, was represented by those two figures.

We artists are simple and minimalist. Just a little, just what matters. We suffer because we are essentially innocent and full of affection.

Mario Schifano's painting, which is an improvised gesture that transforms into colour, has affected my dance, which also incorporates this element, the strength of the action. Dance is also painting in movement that changes colour and intensity; in fact, there is colour in movement and sound.

Mario should have designed the scene of my new production *Hyde & Eva*. For the first time I felt the need for a scene to be designed that could create a space suited for the theme of the show, that is, the struggle between good and evil. Until then, the only scenic element of my works had been the lights. The choreographer is also a director because she not only directs her performers, she visualizes and supervises the theatrical elements of the performance, like costumes, lights, music, stage elements. With *Hyde & Eva*, for the first time direction took over choreography, becoming the guiding factor for the creation of movements. With this show, an essential element of innovation was incorporated in my manner of working. It continues to this day.

Unfortunately, it was impossible even professionally to deal with Mario because of his recurrent instability. One day he enthusiastically confirmed his commitment to the project, and then for days he disappeared without even answering the phone. There were only a few months left for the debut at the Teatro Olimpico in Rome, and I didn't know how I would do it because he wasn't making up his mind about creating the scene. I talked about it with my dear friend, Simonetta Lux, a renowned historian of contemporary art and teacher at the Sapienza University of Rome. She had the brilliant idea to introduce me to Fabio Mauri, the giant of the Italian avant-garde. I visited Fabio Mauri at his home in Piazza Navona. He was incredibly charismatic and had a strong and intense personality. He exuded elegance, dignity, culture, refinement and nobility of soul.

I described the project and Fabio listened to me very carefully. He had never created the scene for performances outside of his own, so although he complimented me for what I described, which he said he had found compelling and intriguing, he did not accept the collaboration and elegantly dismissed me.

The next morning, very early, the telephone rang.

"Patrizia, if you accept the challenge, tonight I have done the sketch for the scene of your show," he told me.

"Fabio, I accept the challenge, whatever it is," I replied.

So it was. I believe no choreographer would have accepted that challenge.

Fabio had cluttered the scene with rough, empty packing boxes, so that we had room to dance. We had to recapture the action moment by moment, by moving them according to our needs and thus making the scene take on different forms. Some of the boxes were reinforced so that we could dance on them. There was also a swing, a ladder, a railing and a few other props.

I used the boxes to depict villages, roads, caverns to seek refuge in, pedestals to dance on, barriers to surmount and walls to tear down. For a show that dealt with good and evil, it was perfect!

Lightness and spirituality are the purity of the emptiness; I was not yet aware of the necessity to symbolize the bad accumulations in the unconscious when I offered the proposal to him. He instinctively understood that. It was a very spectacular image that seemed both real and otherworldly.

At the start of the project I rushed to Mario to tell him all that had happened. "Careful", he muttered in a low voice, "because he will make the usual sarcophaguses for you." Rivalry between artists?

"Perhaps", I replied, "but what a brilliant scene; a true masterpiece!"

A precious partnership was thus born between Fabio and me. He came to the rehearsals every day which was more than necessary. He enjoyed being present to witness each stage of the work's creative process, and his presence gave me strength and inspiration.

I have never used my dreams for my creations, as Federico Fellini used to do. To bring the adventures of my dreams in the creative realm of reality by putting them on stage as art would have been a poor replica of them. The oneiric and artistic processes are not the same, and I have always chosen to keep them separate because I already dream with open eyes while I create and live in reality.

While you are dreaming, just like when you are creating, the witness is active; this is why you remember dreams as well as everything that is born in your imagination. The soul captures the core of the dream's direct, powerful and pure experience, which is beyond the mind and the body. The dream is an end in itself.

Intuition, like the dream, belongs to the unconscious, but while creating art, mind and body are involved as tools. This process cannot take place in a dream, hence it is not like creating art, but something else.

Those who have a ceaseless relationship with the dream life can also stimulate dreams in others, as happened between me and Fabio Mauri. One day Fabio arrived at the rehearsal and described a dream he had had the previous night: I had entered the scene with strength and determination, and I grabbed a man by his genitals and spun him around in somersaults and cartwheels. I immediately created a choreography exactly like that, but no, don't worry!

The dancer, wearing a black military outfit and a short black wig, was in a harness on stage, and a rope sprang from it. I grabbed it and spun it around as I pleased, acrobatically. Massimiliano Martoriati, the well-known TV dancer in prime-time shows, was my partner. He was gorgeous and strong. We had fun unleashing ourselves and being excessive in our sado-masochistic transgression which shook the astonished audience, and had them on edge as if I was holding the extension of each of them in my hands. The show *Hyde & Eva* was a resounding success.

6

The Creative Process

Like everything else, art also arises from tumult, from chaos.

My way of dancing is to get into a state of profound devotion, total surrender, as if it were an offering, a gift of beauty to the cosmos, to God. I am one with the movement that expresses itself through me; I become the channel for the flow. I lose myself in it and then find myself again. I become the instrument of communication with the same depth and brilliance from where it originates. I feel the power of this magical synthesis between dance, me and the spectator who comes out of it transformed, whether he realizes it or not. When one enters the water, one emerges wet. How many times in life have you become involved without knowing it, and still enjoy the precious fruits, without realizing it?

When I dance, I always keep my eyes in Shambhavi mudra open but looking inwards. I am the witness. Even today dancing makes me experience the state of inner bliss, accompanied by a sense of peace and weightlessness, in which I feel the satisfaction of being the real me. Outside, I experience the beauty of movement, in which my body finds its "lightness". The desire to recreate this joy has given me and continues to give me the strength to persevere, overcoming all difficulties and barriers.

At the age of eighteen I started composing choreographies. I attended a choreography course and created a piece in silence in which I portrayed *La Pazzia di Ophelia* (The Madness of Ophelia) from Shakespeare. This was an expressive solo, made up of a few movements in which the body abandons itself in the void, as happens in madness, where the sense of abandonment springs from the suffering that I could only sublimate in dance. I was able to express the state in which one completely loses oneself, even one's consciousness, as in madness. On the one hand, you feel a deep fear and anguish, as if you were in a nightmare, totally naked and alone in a storm without any protection.

On the other hand, you also feel you have the privilege of surrendering to poetry and the beauty of living without any constraints that come from consciousness.

Immediately afterwards, I choreographed a piece from Igor Stravinsky's *Histoire Du Soldat*, "Marche!" In white tights, white face with accentuated large black eyes, the interpreter, usually a man on toe tips, moves rhythmically, creating lines and angles that involve all parts of the body. In the end he falls to the ground backwards, stiff like a puppet, to be carried away by two attendants. The professor's reaction was one of great surprise for the peculiarity of the movements and the originality of the language. This was the first time a choreographer could demonstrate ironical rigidity through the creation of angles in each segment of the body, synchronized with the richness of its dynamics.

At that time, I also created a piece inspired by Kafka's *Metamorphosis*. The de-structuring of the human body in this solo performance caused the interpreter, Patrizia Macagno, with whom I mounted it to experience the feel of an animal's movement. The choreography began with the body locked and coiled up on the floor, both legs over the head and all the weight on the shoulders, while only one hand could be moved in a restricted way. This was followed by rolling to one side, making it very hard to stand up, or take steps with the legs.

With those early experiences, the essential characteristics of my dance language emerged: strong, interpretative, expressive, fluid and fluent, with the dynamics of movements that synchronize, making all parts of the body, including the hair, move audaciously. I know I am volcanic and when my ideas erupt, I must immediately carve out a channel for the creative lava that flows out; otherwise it becomes uncontrollable and implosive.

If you ask me how I prefer to dance, I would say in silence, naked like truth.

The truth is difficult to sustain, even more than beauty and goodness because it is not easily recognizable. We often live in falsehoods without even realizing it. It is not easy to see the mystery that is within us, to face the darkness in which to bring light. It is in that light which illuminates the truth that one sleeps and lives, serenely.

During the process of creation an artist is absorbed in the Absolute. For this to happen, she must be focused on a total abandonment, where the masculine and the feminine, the rational and the unconscious unite. When I choreograph, my tools are the dancers, who are one with me at that moment and completely immersed in this magical, floating-in-the-air sensation and the enchanting process. On the human level, I loved all my dancers and I chose them based on their erotic intensity. Eros, the expression of the soul through the body, has to be awakened.

The dancers are the pen, the sheet, the canvas and the colours, the score and the strings. In my next life, I would rather have one of them as a tool than a human dancer because humans are too human exhausting and difficult to handle. It is hard to be a choreographer because in addition to dealing with all your own inner resistances, you must also manage the dancers' universe.

Actually, the work of art already exists and we artists unearth it from the depths where it lies hidden. In the creative act, we realize the fusion of opposites, of the masculine and feminine elements, in an alchemical process that transmutes everything to gold. Just as there is only elevation and purity when the ideal relationship between man and woman, is realized. The difficulty in reaching the summit in human relationships arises from the inability to accept the other's uniqueness and limitations with tolerance and love, without ever compromising. In artistic creation, as in life, one has to win over the fear of the void.

Inspiration that dwells in the cosmic and divine dimension, is a seed that, when planted in fertile ground, germinates and allows the birth of artistic work. It is a profoundly spiritual creative process that rises to rejoin the divine from where it originated, now transformed into a work of art.

Creativity is a descending and ascending flow that can occur in anyone who wants it, but only under certain conditions. The first condition, a sine qua non, concerns talent. Artists are born, not made. For those who believe in the renewal of life through time and reincarnations of being, genius is simply the accumulation of talents acquired in prior lifetimes over time and space.

They are the karmic seeds that settle in the unconscious, only to be revealed through the elaboration over time in the experiential life. For those who do not recognize in themselves the law of karma, genius remains essentially a mystery.

In my experience, the second condition is the willingness to accept inspiration that enters the unconscious in the depths of the belly, where intuition, instinctive impulses and the will reside. The seed needs fertile soil to germinate, grow and yield fruit. Humus is needed: that is humility, receptivity, passive surrender and active self-giving. The artist unconsciously prepares the ground by combining the elements that will make the creation phase possible, then comes the moment of inspiration in which the seed is planted.

In order for the creative process to overcome inner enemies such as insecurity, a feeling of unworthiness and the fear of failing, the right conditions must be created for its ascent into the vertical flow. All this can be real labour.

But when the work emerges, free to be itself and beautiful in its completeness, it is a feast in the cosmos, on earth as in heaven! All beings vibrate with that joy, artists and spectators united by love, all the strings stretched in unison to project souls into the highest vibrations, into the excellence of living.

What is more beautiful for an artist than having the power to transport her audience up there with her? How lucky I have been!

The divine gift can potentially touch any human being, but it is only to those who are able to reunite with the creativity bestowed upon them by divine inspiration. It is a process that can also cause the artist both pain and fear. The experience of that pain is so strong that it becomes unbearable.

It is not by chance that those with talent live through phases during which they are susceptible, even prone to attempt suicide. The artist absorbs life's emotions to the point of completely internalizing them, then gets to know their essence from which she creates the symbols and signs through which to express that essence in her work. When applied to the human dimension, the process transforms the artist into a true shaman, absorbing the pain of others and guiding them through an alchemical self-healing process.

Absorbing is different from suffering because one is conscious of the process; otherwise one undergoes suffering. The artist is an expert in suffering pain. That is why she knows how to descend into the abyss, absorb the energy and the thrust there, and rise to a dimension above life and reality, above joy and pain, and in this way, becoming fit to survive.

Creating art becomes an artist's *boccata d'aria*, the coming up for air. But this is not the way to resolve suffering at its root. Art cannot do that. The true artist lives those ups and downs with such intensity that art becomes a drug, a palliative for suffering, the only way she has to escape the torture that life can be.

If the artist wants to get out of the vicious circle of pain, she must break this chain in life, in its human dimension. Artists often presume that the creative process is also therapeutic. Not only that, art is also the great seductress. Like a snake that bites its tail in an act of unwitting self-infliction, as in seduction, an act in which one is doing more harm to oneself than the other. Isn't life itself a seduction?

I have been through the tunnel of life and pain. The chain of pain must be broken by working on oneself. Breaking it means having the courage to emerge from the vortex of suffering by confronting, understanding and resolving within oneself, the deep and unconscious causes, the emotional blocks created by one's way of reacting to events. The artist must have the humility to recognize that in order to overcome these psychoses, which originate in the inner conflict of the ego with the self, and are sometimes even useful as an impulse for artistic creativity, she must move into a therapeutic dimension.

The artist is clearly an expert in suffering because she has a big ego, which she should not be ashamed of, nor be demonized for. The ego is also the reason why she is extremely sensitive and therefore suffers. Everyone should undergo a therapeutic-spiritual journey to preserve their life by breaking free from the trap of contemplative and self-congratulatory egoism.

Inspiration clashes with matter; the human ego is afraid of dying by surrendering to the divine, and I can affirm that it is from this very fear that sorrow arises. Vulnerability is strength, not a weakness. It is only to greatly fragile hearts that God gives everything. To truly live, one must first know how to die.

It is not easy or even simple to manage the gift of art: you are aware that you are, in your art, one with God, that you are born with the mark of that union. It is an awareness that can be expressed on the slippery slope of arrogance and pride, a claim to independence from the divine and self-affirmation of these privileges, as happened to the angel Lucifer before his fall from grace. Rudolf Steiner, the noted philosopher, said that the artist is like Lucifer, the angel closest to God, the bearer of His light. He was also the angel who entered into conflict with God, and as a result of his choices, caused his own fall to the underworld,

The creative experience is so intense and powerful that it becomes extremely difficult to deal with it in the human dimension. An artist's excessive humanity puts him at risk of being drawn into the self-destructive and transgressive vortex, a ferocious process that can lead to the most dramatic extremes: drugs, drink and suicide. At best, the risk is that she falls into a manic-depressive state of which she is not in the least aware, thereby becoming a vampire for those around him. For this reason, Steiner observed, few artists rise above it, while the majority remain slaves, victims of the divine gift.

It is even more difficult for the artist to find God in the human dimension, but it is precisely there that He hides, and in order to come out from the abyss, the artist must be humble, accept her own smallness and her insignificance. It is difficult for an artist to achieve true humility, not the one suggested by reason but the deep and visceral one, especially when she is successful and is treated like a god.

What I am about to say is very bold, it is something that characterizes both me and my life: The artist lives too much in the truth, to the point of not tolerating those human actions which arise from falsehood. Therefore, the artist escapes into art.

"Feeling" is the strongest element of my existence. Things vibrate in the depths and I feel them. As I was dissatisfied with my work and success, my existential crisis at the age of twenty-eight was the trigger that prompted me to seek spiritual awakening in India.

Before, I was a textbook artist, full of transgression, self-destruction, a conscious choice that was born from my ego, from narcissism, from the self-satisfaction of pain. I was willing to do anything to find myself again, even stop dancing. I had often suspended my activities, even given up on success: interviews, a good life, admirers showering me with flowers and gifts, dedications and poems, and everything you can imagine.

I came out of pain thanks to India that pulled me back by the hair and that was my salvation. It ignited in me the energy with which I broke the deadly chain. My whole life was a search for the balance between the spiritual and the human dimension, between the artist and the woman, between the masculine and feminine element, within me. To seek, to find.

When the artist places herself as a researcher, and therefore an experimenter, she denies her inner need for truth to live, to vibrate/pulsate. The real artist does not feel she is the author while she creates. I have no doubt that true art happens like this. Like a child that must be born, because it has its own unconscious, deep and spiritual path. It is not you, but it is the cosmos that brings you that inspiration, you are merely a tool. You are one with the cosmos.

However, the researcher becomes self-conscious as an author; she does not go beyond the narcissistic impulse, focusing more in craft and technique. That is not to suggest that genius cannot exist in the craftsperson if the same process as the artist's is awakened in her. But the converse can also happen—the artist loses the original tension and her work becomes a mere handicraft. That is quite possible.

The mastery of the artisan lies in making something useful, where external beauty is an end in itself. In art what really matters is not the superficial beauty, but the truth that dwells within it. This is the difference between an artist and a craftsman.

When the expression of an inner content passes through the strokes of the painter's brush on the canvas, the sounds of a musical instrument, movements of a dancer or the words of a poet, it acquires meaning and reaches the essence of beauty, which lies deep in the heart. With the craftsman, such beauty does not spring from these inner depths because it is only external.

An artist's intention is to dive into the mystery. The will is to bring out what pulsates within, the vibration that originates from the depth that has the strength to connect with the interiority of the audience. The true artist is not moved by the ambition to succeed but by the strength of the love within her. The art itself is unaffected by how the artist uses it, but as with everything else, it all depends on the attitude with which one lives. This is in fact what the artistic process is. Tantrism teaches the same process in the erotic-sexual-spiritual dimensions.

The artist works in the vertical, which is the line of union between the unconscious and the highest spirituality. It is in the vertical, the path that allows the artist to reach the unconscious root of the soul, to elaborate it, purify it, bring it up to consciousness. The fertile soil, the humus that attracts it, is in the unconscious. The full spiritual realization, the fusion with God, happens when the unconscious roots where the karmic seeds reside with their history have been purified in the earthly existence.

The artist is the medium of that seed, which she alone understands and interprets, much like a mother does with her child. When a life is being born within you, you feel it, listen to it, understand it and, above all, nourish it. The artist does the same, she has it inside and must understand how and when the work will choose to be released, and what form it will take.

At the time of the creation of the work, the artist enters the horizontal, that is, the physical dimension of the material; the form that takes shape is its body. The artist strives to achieve the perfect balance between the physical/horizontal plane and the unconscious/ spiritual plane for the game of existence is all about this balance.

My logo which I like to call the symbol of the sun, represents the meeting point between the vertical and the horizontal, right there, in the heart. The greatest mystery in this symbol is that the vertical line is formed by the legs, one in line over the other, the horizontal by the arms which open like wings. The legs in which the realization of the will resides, are required to rise in the vertical, the spiritual sphere, while the arms through which the soul is expressed, the inner world of sensations, feelings, emotions, must stretch in the horizontal, the realm of the material and the real world.

There is so much love in that act of surrender on the horizon inspired from above, which runs through the heart like the offering of the self. The gaze is focused to maintain the balance in the precariousness of human existence, always between dream and reality, rational and irrational, power and surrender, failure and success.

It is amazing for me to see how the artist, through symbols and signs, discovers profound truths that he will understand only in time, as if only time could bring to full awareness the truths contained in them. I see in the unconscious dimension as you see in the light of the sun. My "finding" in life is a process that will never end. My life is the aspiration to realize the union of the spirit and matter at the point of the heart as in the cross, the meeting point between the horizontal and the vertical.

According to the philosophy of rebirth every soul undergoes a purification process depending on the karma it has collected in the previous birth, only then does it reincarnate into another life on earth. Some people are born artists because the process of purification has been accomplished karmically to the point of being able to reconnect with that higher creativity. That does not mean that they are more advanced than others as human beings, but they are so in creativity that they can see beyond reality. I believe that even in life, only when this process of purification has been completed can we rise again in the spiritual dimension from which we have come. The soul incarnates from the afterlife and descends to earth.

The purpose of this book is to make not just artists but all those who experience the same elemental creative turmoil understand that this is in fact their essential and unique value

Ancient cultures knew and respected this when it came to developing unique skills that were beneficial to society when encouraging and enhancing the rare skills/talents. Today these values are not only misunderstood, but also trampled, ghettoized, commercialized.

For everyone, the body is the instrument of the soul. Just as a musician needs an instrument, my body is my instrument in dance. Every artistic expression incorporates the spiritual, physical, unconscious, mental and emotional dimensions. The dance starts from the body to express them all—the body, not the brush or the canvas, not the violin or the voice! Dance is pure poetry in which the colour of painting, the plasticity of sculpture, the space of architecture and the rhythm of poetry come together.

In dance it is not the positions of departure and arrival of movements that make the body speak, but the dynamic that is expressed between them. It is in the movement that the body speaks. I am not interested in facts but in the dynamics that move them because it is there that emotion, eroticism and life are expressed.

What is higher than sound that is seen and not heard?

What is more intense than the sound that lives through silence and the stillness of movement?

The energy that is unleashed in the stillness of a dancer is greater than the energy that will be released a moment later in the movement. It is a symbolic and creative contraction and compression before the explosion.

What is more powerful than the instant just before, which is suspension and silence?

Now, finally, I am ready to even love, accept and forgive my own way of being human.

I consider myself truly fortunate to be a woman whose greatest achievement has been the successful realization of spirituality through the human dimension.

7

Life on Tour

Dance is a language of the body. The interpreter must assimilate it, internalize it, make it her own and then speak through it.

I founded my own dance company because having dancers who understood my language allowed me to create my choreographies with them.

It is essential that the choreographers shape their own interpreters because not all dancers who come from other dance techniques, particularly those who have only performed classical ballet, can easily adapt to another style. They find my language of movement extremely difficult because it forces them to dismantle their rigid armour-like style and adapt to the fluidity of contemporary dance. The interpreter learns the language by working directly with the choreographer, step by step. It is not like music, which can be written, and hence studied and applied by reading it. Dance does not offer this option.

The very first formation of my dance company Patrizia Cerroni & I Danzatori Scalzi (The Barefoot Dancers) was created with the teachers of the Academy and artists who were chosen during my workshops.

I offered courses for professionals at I.A.L.S. Dance Studio, some of whom were the best television dancers of the time as well as some promising new talents of contemporary dance. I selected the ones most suitable to the canons of my style. I rarely held auditions because I did not think it right to form an opinion about an interpreter in just a few hours. Since I had to assess a large number of them, I needed personalized, intimate meetings in order to get to know the talent and expressiveness of each dancer.

For me, the best way to choose interpreters has always been during my courses, when I could observe them while they were studying. That was the only way I could determine who could travel professionally with me.

Each new dance production needs months of rehearsals, at least eight hours a day. It is not like composing music, where you study the score and then gather for a few days of rehearsals. I have no script, I "write" the roles on the dancers' bodies in the rehearsal room. The notes are the moving bodies.

Cunningham has created a program to write choreographies on a computer, but I don't use it because I don't think the same results are produced. The dance is "in the here and now" because the body exists at the time it is created. It is born and dies a moment after it is born. This is anti-computer, anti-technology.

Dance is complex, especially contemporary dance, which moves a thousand cells of the body simultaneously. It is impossible to describe how all parts of the body move simultaneously and in different ways.

The work of the choreographer is intricate, complex and tricky because, in addition to creating the work, she must guide the dancers through their own creative process as interpreters. The choreographer must travel along with them, through the blocks and the difficulties they might face in becoming one with the movement created by her. For the choreographer, dancers are the tools but not like the brushes and colours of the painter, or the pens and words of the poet. The dancers are human, animate, thinking and feeling beings, with their own needs and concerns. They cannot be taken for granted. One must learn to deal with them sensitively.

I always encouraged my dancers to interact with other choreographers. I was the complete opposite of those possessive colleagues who wanted to keep the dancers all to themselves. I urged them to experiment with others because an artist must be open to new experiences and willing to take risks. This is also true in life.

I loved my dancers as a mother loves her children, and I think I was a good mother to them because I did everything I could to help them grow and progress, not just as artists but also as human beings. I enjoyed our journeys together, and I am satisfied with what we have achieved. Even today, I feel a deep connection with them, after years of our last collaboration. We are kindred spirits.

Our interaction was conducted with full awareness of the roles. I always told them in the rehearsal room, "With me you play but you don't joke around". Outside of work, I sometimes let my guard down with them.

Even Guido was loved by everyone; in fact, he was loved much more than me. He was the good cop while I was the bad one. Are you laughing at me? I am sure you know this is not true, but I had to discipline them for their own good.

Just a few days ago, a former assistant of mine, Malvina Cirelli, sent me some photos while she was having dinner with six former dancers of the Barefoot Dancers and the formation *Hyde & Eva* and *Folli d'amori* shows. It was like stepping back twenty years in time to see them so happy and smiling, despite the fact that some of them had gained a few extra pounds, while others were in wonderful shape. The caption of the photos read: "It seems that time has not passed; every time we meet, we experience the same joy and creativity as when we worked together with you".

The remarkable coincidence was that I had gone to the Fabio Mauri Foundation the previous evening for an event commemorating his tenth death anniversary, when there had been talks of performing *Hyde & Eva* again which, as you know, included his scene with the boxes.

It seemed like a sign from the heavens! So I replied to Cirelli's message: "Are you ready to play *Hyde & Eva* again after losing a few pounds?"

I thought it would be great to reassemble the show with the original performers who were more artistically mature now. In India, in fact, older dancers are appreciated, loved and respected: what matters is not their physical appearance but what emanates from them.

I handled my company in a dynamic and free manner. The free artist is enthusiastic, creative, fulfils herself with courage, and does not accept compromises and constraints. If a soul is rooted in poetry, harmony and freedom, it moves like a dancer. The lightness of the body depends on the soul. The masters are the ones who awaken what is hidden in such souls. I probably brought to light some dimensions of my dancers that otherwise would not have been discovered. When an interpreter understands the language of the choreographer, she, that is the dancer/ interpreter, is stimulated to enter into her own creative process, if she has the potential to be a choreographer herself.

Many of my dancers have gone on to become choreographers and have founded their own companies. Working with me prepared them for choreographic composition; it was the springboard for their careers. I can confidently affirm that many of contemporary Italian dancers have grown with me. I am proud to say that they have all had wonderful careers.

I have always told my dancers, "Live the present moment that passes and dissolves in all its splendour, to give space and time to the next present moment that passes and dissolves ... and so on ... suspended and surrendered, in detachment, in the infinite, like a drop that finds itself in water. The art of living illuminates the mystery, the movement vibrates in the inner light. "

In my madness as an artist, I have often felt the strong impulse to reset everything to zero and start from the beginning. It is undoubtedly exhausting, but it is also regenerative; we rise again and again to fresh life, like the phoenix from the ashes.

I also did it with the various formations of Barefoot Dancers. In its forty-year history, I have recreated at least ten new groups from scratch because like jazz groups which are fluid formations and collaborate only on a project basis since their hallmark is improvisation and individual expression, so it is with my dance. As I have already stated, I love everything that is in constant motion, such as transformation, renovation.

I could go into details of the inner world of each of the three hundred professional dancers and thousands of students who studied and worked with me but I will mention only a few, without taking anything away from the others, who also I have deeply loved. Dancers who were artists but also narcissistic and prima donnas enriched me with their talent, while others such as Giovanni Romeo and Rosanna Maggio, enriched me also with their humanity. Some had only humanity but were able to compensate for their lack of true talent on the stage with their sincerity and compassion. Last but not least, I will not reveal the identities of the dancers I fell in love with since there would be too many, even if they never became my lovers. I am against mixing work with emotional involvement.

I am bound to Giovanni Romeo by deep friendship, which I knew instinctively even then, would develop between us. An architect, originally from Messina in Sicily, he chose to live in Catania where the immense energy of the active volcano Etna and the energy of the sea come together to enhance the city's own energy. Energy which everyone there can sense.

Catania saw the debut of The Barefoot Dancers in 1974. It was Giovanni's father who introduced me to Gioacchino Lanza Tommasi, artistic director of Taormina Art's Festival, one of Sicily's premier cultural events, which included my shows in the festival program.

In the many decades of my dancing career, I have performed at almost all the festivals and theatres of Sicily, which is noted for its culture and natural beauty. More than forty civilizations settled here, leaving an indelible mark on the inhabitants. In them, I find my preferred audience. Sicilians, thanks to their culture and nature, are incredibly erotic. That is probably why I believe they are the best audience for my dance.

In fact, Giovanni surrounded himself with a large circle of friends creating an atmosphere reminiscent of Almodovar's movies, in which people come together to support one another with love, acceptance and, when required, forgiveness.

Today, like then, I cherish his friendship for these very qualities.

Patrizia Macagno, one of the greatest dancers of my company who was also my assistant, is one of those who became a choreographer and founded a company of her own with other former Barefoot Dancers. Our collaboration has never ceased, in art as in life: a friendship that has lasted for over fifty years. Although we are diametrically opposite, we can always find harmony and mutual understanding between us.

We attended the Academy together. We have known each other since we were teenagers, little women already mature and independent. Dance makes one grow quickly thanks to the tough discipline and the complete concentration it constantly demands. Patrizia has always given strength, stability and solidarity to me. She is open, loyal, intelligent, full of energy with a smile on her face and deep green kind eyes. Even today, she is a concrete and rational woman, guided by a clear intuition.

This is also true of her dance style.

Athletic, slender, linear, in the movement more powerful than fluid, she is like a precise blade that cuts the air. In the Academy at the year-end essay the director decided to cast the two of us from two different courses in a duet rather than a solo for each of us. We danced in unison with ease and true friendship, having fun and with satisfaction. I involved Patrizia in all my projects, and she participated with great enthusiasm and energy: we are two terrific workers who never knew how to say enough. Ah, dance! Not only does it raise the soul, but it vigorously strengthens all the dimensions of being.

Laura Morante, the famous actress, was just twenty years old when she was introduced to me by a friend of a friend whom I respected. I liked her personality, intensity, and the unique and rare beauty of her face and neck, which reminded me of Modigliani's models. Although, she did not always know quite what to do with her body. Above all, the dancer is an actor; in my emotional dance, the interpretation of the movement counts, so I immediately accepted Laura into the company.

I never chose dancers based on their physical appearance or technical abilities, even though I have had beautiful and talented ones. I chose a dancer because of her capacity to portray her inner world and deep feelings. Even the so-called ugly can display beauty and personality that distinguish them from those considered beautiful, who perhaps let themselves be conditioned and crushed by the conventional aesthetic standards.

It was 1976 and once again I was rebuilding The Barefoot Dancers from scratch. I had moved from a group formed with highly technical teachers from the Academy, who were unable to connect with their inner dimension, to a group consisting of Enrica Palmieri, Laura Morante, Paolo Morelli, Hal Yamanouchi, and other young people full of will and expressiveness, with artistic rather than technical abilities.

When the Italian actor, poet, film director and screenwriter Carmelo Bene came to see me with Michelangelo Antonioni, and noticed Laura, he immediately fell in love with her and involved her in his show *Riccardo III* (1977). Laura rehearsed with me until the evening, and with him until late at night. She was dedicated to her job; she never gave up, she held up any effort, any challenge, even those that I created myself. I made life difficult, not only for her, but also for myself. I am afraid I was fierce with all my dancers, but they thank me for it.

I loved her but kept it a secret, and only wanted the best for her. She was quite sweet when she tried movements she couldn't perform; like a puppy she lost her balance and recovered, focusing to retry shyly. Laura made the dance her own, but she didn't entirely abandon herself until she lost herself in it and became one with it. The letting go to which I allude is, for all of us, the most difficult achievement in this life.

It must reach the point of surrendering totally to the love that is deep within. Laura's inner world was intense, emphasizing technique, on the elasticity of the body, on the dynamism. Who knows, maybe Laura should have continued to dance!

Laura was always kind and helpful to everyone, humble and collaborative with the other dancers who loved her. Passionate about literature, she often quoted from her readings and as a good Tuscan, she was sharp and sardonic despite her youth. Laura once told me, "You are as strong as Gargantua and Pantagruel put together." Remembering her words, helped me in difficult moments to believe in myself and my ability to overcome adversity.

She once said to the others in my presence, "Guido is not her half but her double", and I don't think she meant his height! What *did* you mean, Laura?

In another situation, she stated, "Better a good mother than a bad boss" while comparing her experience with me to that with Carmelo Bene. Laura and I were only a few years apart, but I guess calling me mother was a compliment, given how demanding I was with her. She also said, "We are not the poor ones, she is, she must endure herself twenty-four hours a day!"

She had hit the mark! I was asking too much of myself, of others and of life. This happened before I went to India. After India, everything changed: now it is much worse, I ask for the impossible, pure love at all times.

Laura and I had a deep connection—she made me feel understood. When I quit smoking, she saw me struggling. She invited me to her small family house in the mountains of Maremma. During our stay, I remember washing our clothes in the lavatorio, the square's washhouse, alongside the local housewives, which was something I had never done before.

Laura's persona fostered a sense of inadequacy and shyness. In truth, she was extremely strong and confident. She comes across as insecure but she is the complete opposite. I consider her behaviour psychoanalytically false. With me, Laura assumed the attitude of submission without realizing it, while I sensed her determination. We were in conflict because of this game that she played with herself and with me. I believe her behaviour was a kind of a mask. That was her problem.

Laura worked with me for only a couple of years, participating in many productions and also taking part in the tour of the sports palaces of Italy and in Cannes with the rock band Banco Del Mutuo Soccorso, when the famous music impresario David Zard commissioned me to do the choreographies for *Come in un'ultima cena* (As in the Last Supper). She participated in *Orpheus and Eurydice* by C. W. Gluck and *Creation du Monde* (Creation of the World) to Darius Milhaud's music, which I developed for Swiss TV in Lugano with the orchestra Music Ensemble of Cremona, and in many other projects. With great affection, I followed her career as a successful actress, as she attested to mine with her presence at my opening nights.

Tights were almost exclusively utilized as costumes for modern dance in the 1970s, and I did the same at first. Guido and Francesco Marconi, an architect friend, painted images from the grotesque illustrations in Jurgis Baltrusaitis' medieval book *Medioevo Fantastico* on the black tights for *Apotropia*, a choreography based on Frank Zappa's *Chunga's Revenge*. The images included masks, dragons and snakes in vibrant hues, evoking the force of our movements.

When I went to India and created *Tendrils and my dreams echoed with his melodies*, I was compelled to expand the spandex by extending it below the knee, allowing the movement to be extended in the costume. For the first time I designed the costumes myself, which I got made by the tailors of Delhi.

Back in Rome I met Dino Orlando, who had returned to Italy after around forty years in New York, where he had dressed famous stars and celebrities including Jacqueline Kennedy. He worked for various *prêt-à-porter* houses in northern Italy as a fashion designer. He personally chose the fabrics in Biella, the city of wool, before the dramatic collapse of the textile industry, as fabrics are now purchased in China because they are cheaper, undoubtedly of poor quality. This is how the excellent Italian quality is gradually dying in many fields.

Dino felt passionately about my dance and we became close friends. A collaboration was formed, resulting in a very experimental piece on how to outfit the dancer. He designed the costumes for many of my shows using clothing inspired by everyday life, which was ideal for my contemporary dance. For *Divertissement Lyrique* (a French expression meaning an entertaining lyrical interlude), a show with only female dancers and two musicians, he created a costume that I think is a masterpiece: warm gold-coloured silk almost like a palazzo pajama, with overlaps that fly and vibrate like butterflies on the front.

With Marco Stagi, the young man who had recently graduated from the Academy of Costume, we used plastic for the first time as a material. On the occasion of *Ladies and Gentlemen*, he created amazing skirts for the female dancers with transparent plastic tight at the waist like a tutu, with flame-like yellow-orange-red streaks that gave the illusion of fire. I had a dream in which the male dancers appeared with bands on their chests indicating physical power, and a thick cotton material descended from the belt like a third leg. Marco recreated for the men exactly what I had seen in the dream. It was very effective on stage.

The experimentation continued with the high fashion house Piano Piano Dolce Carlotta (Slow, slow sweet Carlotta) for the *Hyde & Eva* show. The stylist was Antonio Marras, a versatile artist. While Dino created the costumes specifically for me, Marras' fashion house gave me the opportunity to choose from the collections. It was an honour and also very exciting to select any dress of that creative level and high-quality craftsmanship from a warehouse of 500 square metres. I had a lot of fun with high fashion, and I hope I didn't disappoint Marras by choosing minimalist and essential clothes.

The same was true for Sem Vaccaro, an unconventional and audacious stylist, who generously let me use his warehouses in the *Marche for*

Tosca—The Power against Love and *Cleopatra—The Power of Love*. Given that these presentations featured two prominent female figures, I opted for rich and grand costumes for the first time.

Clothes the dancers wear undoubtedly contributed significantly to my dance, imbuing it with contemporary and emotional strength. But for a dance in which every cell of the body is an instrument of movement, nudity is ideal. I have often danced naked; however, I have never been able to convince my dancers to do it with me. It is not easy for everyone to do. Nakedness is freedom, anything worn while dancing is cumbersome.

In a percussion piece set to the overture of *Folli d'amori*, I danced naked in a role that evoked the image of a warrior unleashed on the battlefield, with my integral nudity visible against the backlight.

The original concept for *Ma volete capire qualcosa di noi donne??!!!* (But you want to understand anything about us women??!!!) was for my partner Corrado Celestini and me to dance naked in an erotic pas de deux to Leonard Cohen's warm voice.

However, at some point during the rehearsals, Corrado began to slowly convince me that he would never be able to support that entirely naked part on stage; it was different in practice.

Nearing his debut, he finally admitted his total inability. I didn't know what to do. At that point, I felt as if Dino Orlando, whom we had lost a few years earlier, had come to my aid from heaven. It seemed as if he was throwing me an Indian sari to work with. It was a brilliant idea.

I remember we were working in my open space in Viale Libia, where I lived and where I would create many other shows in the coming years. All the furniture was on wheels so shifting them towards the entrance gave us free space in a matter of minutes. This was one of the most suitable houses I lived in because we artists need a lot of empty space around. Certainly, heavily furnished houses are warmer but we need to find the heat inside not outside.

The die was cast! Inspired by Dino, I dashed to my room and retrieved a turquoise silk sari from a drawer. I played on the heightened contrast, between myself, naked, and Corrado in formal coat and tails with the turquoise silk fabric between us, which he used to cover and reveal me. The sari was difficult to handle because though it was more than six metres long, it had to fly with me. But Corrado was prepared to do anything as long as he could go on stage fully clothed!

I was very surprised by the reaction of the public and the comments in the dressing room after the show: the men looked intimidated and didn't speak to me, while the women complimented me enthusiastically. They had identified themselves with that dance and I think I understood why. The choreography expresses the way in which women like to be loved—in full abandonment, in total nakedness of the body/soul. Man must love us through our bodies in the full nakedness of his heart, so he can also remain clothed.

For both Corrado and myself, this dance aroused in our human dimension what we were expressing in the choreography, namely our eroticism.

The two levels, human and creative, overlapped, making us believable on stage. We looked like we were lovers in real life as well; many spectators even sought confirmation. Outside of rehearsal, we continued to experience the love we lived in dance and it was not easy for us to maintain those strong impulses on the platonic plane.

The loves that are not consummated are the most intense because we recognize each other through the game of souls, without the distraction of the body. Sometimes the body can become an impediment to love because it makes lovers sink into carnal desire instead of remaining an instrument for realizing that union, as it happens when we dance.

The artist wishes to transmit her art to all. This is a natural, instinctive impulse. The stage is an oasis from the tensions of life, because the strings force one's own and the audience's emotions to vibrate, allowing them to be guided and inspired by what happens. I don't think there is a love greater than this for me. The audience is the ideal lover with whom I can bare my soul. When I am on stage, I feel like a citizen of the world because I love everyone. That is why my life is wonderful!

When we are on tour we live in a state of focus and concentration, where we are ever ready to attract and absorb the essence of our surroundings. We have no time or energy to see anything of the places where we perform, but we know their essence well, especially through our interactions with the audience. The exchange touches the intimate strings that make each person know the other with the same intensity that awakens love.

I'll now share with you some of the most memorable moments from my career.

The brothers David and Dory Zard, renowned promoters of rock/pop music, discovered me while I was just starting out as a choreographer. David and Dory immediately recognized my talent and commissioned me to do the choreography for *Come in un'ultima cena* (As in the Last Supper) by the Italian progressive rock band Banco del Mutuo Soccorso.

Both of them are my closest friends in show business. I am fond of both and feel a deep connection with them. Like Guido, they were born in Tripoli and their beautiful, sweet and witty mother, a fantastic cook, cooked us wicked couscous dishes that were much loved in our parties in Babuccio.

Dory and David have the same beautiful deep blue eyes, which reflect the sea and the sun. Both were intense, cheerful, respectful, rigorously professional and highly creative, albeit with opposite personalities. They knew how to make all artists feel respected; despite being managers and organizers, I have always considered them as artists too.

Living with them was one of the most amazing chapters in my artistic life, along with my tours to India. It was the high levels of energy that was the connection between both these experiences.

My tour with Banco Del Mutuo Soccorso and Angelo Branduardi made me feel like I was in my "perfect waters" and I felt David was right when he said I "rock".

The intensity of our hearts brought us together in the splendid experience in the sports palaces of Italy and Cannes. It was a dangerous time, of upheavals and turmoil, which forced us to have an ambulance behind the stage, just in case.

A director with a crew of five cameramen filmed us all the time, both on stage and back stage. Too bad that all the material shot was lost in some storage shed. I never got to know what really happened, some tangled rock-pop, or "rop" I suppose.

Dory and I have developed a friendship based on lengthy conversations that led to psychoanalytical insights. Together we "split the hairs into sixteen, rather than just four", as we say. We are always there for one another, especially during difficult times. Dory is the ideal companion to travel with in dreams and reality. I remember, in the 1970s he was always dressed in white, regardless of the season.

With David the intensity was the same, but the relationship was far more challenging. Only twenty years later did I realize that, despite our high mutual admiration, the conflicting unconscious dynamic of the manager/artist relationship, for which we were jointly responsible, had started to come between us.

In fact, I recall we were at The Hemingway, a trendy club near Via della Scrofa, to celebrate our debut at Rome's Palazzo dello Sport. David and I sat at a table on our own, drinking champagne, when he said, "Between me and you, there is arm wrestling in which neither one of us will ever give up; we are both too strong to work together".

For me, it was a bolt from the blue. We were in harmony, everything was running smoothly, there had never been the slightest disagreement between us. I love those who can surprise me like this. He had seen beyond appearance. Brilliant. For a young artist, a novice, unaware and unconscious, to hear this from the great manager who brought artists and rock and pop stars from all over the world to Italy! It felt like a David and Goliath situation, in which Goliath was David Zard. His name has a beautiful sound, it represents him as a tsar—he was, tall, strong and emanated a regal presence even in self-mockery.

On the one hand, I was honoured, but on the other I was upset because he was touching on a painful fact that I never gave up, I never relied on anyone and I never trusted anyone. I was tough and determined, I did things my way.

I already knew that I could afford to be free to go wherever my destiny took me, and I treated everyone I met along the road as if they were similarly free, even if they weren't.

Freedom is a big responsibility that people don't want to have. I felt alone when I realized that my freedom was not understood and I had to defend it and make it respected by those who lacked the courage to be free. I would never have let myself be conditioned by a man, and no manager would have been able to do so either. All this was my strength, but also my weakness, the leitmotif of my suffering.

If only David had understood my frailties, had had the strength to reassure me and persuade me to trust him rather than compete with me! Let us hope that instead of the arm wrestling, our magical encounter will be mature enough to become a spiral embrace of souls, from which our masterpiece will emerge.

What do you say David Zard, *will we make it?* I ask you even though you are no longer among us on this wonderful planet. I recall a summer day in Sperlonga. Guido, David, musicians and technicians were playing football on the beach. I, as always, was cocooned in my inner world. It was exhausting to pretend nothing was going on, to pretend to participate, and then to have one part of oneself participate while the other was focused on experiencing and knowing.

How nice to see two seagulls flying in unison!

Life as an artist is intense and hard especially in a culture that does not understand it because it lacks the tools to do so, or has not yet recovered them from that famous golden age when art, artists and women saved the world.

Immediately after that splendid tour, Italo Gomez, the Argentinian musician and director of the prestigious Como Autumn Music Festival, commissioned me to create choreographies for Gluck's *Orfeo and*

Euridice, with repeat performances at the Teatro Grande in Brescia and the Teatro Donizetti in Bergamo. It was an experience opposite to the one with the Zard.

The costumes were heavy, bulky and ridiculous. They should have informed me first about what we would wear to adapt the movements of the choreographies, rather than after everything was done! I rebelled against everything and everybody, creating a lot of tension but without any problem on the professional front because I fulfil my commitments at all costs.

Also, I have never loved the vibrations of an opera house or the attitude with which the salaried workers work, without giving anything of themselves and continually creating problems. One must be motivated to work with enthusiasm but they are not. It doesn't matter what you do in life, what matters is the love you put into it. In this way, every work becomes noble, light and enjoyable.

Thanks to Alberto Testa, famous dancer, choreographer, dance historian and critic, my shows were included on the Teatro Regio's program in Torino. Alberto often spoke with great pride about being able to make such a prominent opera house open its the doors to contemporary dance with my shows. He also included my participation in the Festival of Spoleto when I performed my choreography *Self Mirror* to J. Cage's music.

I surely do not have the vocation of a tourist, but rather that of a monk, for I go throughout the world internalizing everything. That is why every country where I performed my dance was both a challenge and an enrichment for me.

Indians, along with Germans and Americans are my favourite audience. The Indian audience for their openness to everything that comes from the heart, the Germans for their depth of comprehension, the Americans for their enthusiasm that makes them rejoice in everything that has creative value.

I first met Roberto Cavanna, an internationally renowned photographer, in Stockholm, a city that has the unique appeal of cold and frost, which is so well managed and organized that visiting it becomes a pleasant and magical experience. Roberto came to see my show at the Södra Teatern. A very kind, great gentleman, he had lived all his life between New York, Los Angeles and Scandinavia, married and divorced three times, with wives from these countries. He had the courage to leave his important career as a biologist to pursue his passion—photography—in which he excelled.

When he came to see me in the dressing room to ask for permission to photograph the show the next day, it was love at first sight on both the artistic and professional levels for us, a beautiful encounter indeed.

Roberto, a man of great culture and a keen eye like Fabio Mauri, has always been an excellent adviser during rehearsals. He took pictures that showed unexpected nuances, allowing us to grasp the still unseen intensities on which we could work more deeply. He accompanied us on tours whenever he could.

I introduced him to Giacinto Scelsi, a well-known musician who was a friend of mine. He commissioned a photo shoot of his collection of ancient statuettes from different countries. They decided to use my skin as a backdrop, resting them on my body.

Roberto accompanied us on all our tours in Brazil. Through him, on the occasion of our shows at the Theatro Municipal in Rio de Janeiro, I met personalities from the Brazilian artistic world, such as Fernandes Millor, painter, thinker and writer, who gave me one of his books with a humorous dedication "To Patrizia, my new childhood friend", and also the twins Paulo and Chico Caruso, famous caricaturists and performers. Pablo wanted to make me a caricature at one of their highly lively after-show parties, which they held every night.

Who knows how he will transfigure me, I thought, seeing that he was a caricaturist who loved to deform his subjects. It was incredibly nice to see how he portrayed me. He had caught the sweetness of my green eyes, which see beyond, and the softness in my limbs.

We returned to Brazil many times on the invitation of Ambassador Stefano Canavesio, whom I had known years before, when he invited me to perform in Kuala Lumpur. He is an interesting character who, following his diplomatic career, made the courageous choice to live on a boat. After the repeat performance at Simón Bolívar Auditorium in Sao Paulo, we went to dine with his guests of honour—a couple, he was Argentinian and she was British. Enthusiastic about the show, they extended an invitation to the whole company to spend Christmas and New Year in their villa between San Paulo and Rio.

We had returned from a long tour that included dates in New York at the Gala Italia, and I was the only one who accepted the invitation because I wanted to enjoy a luxurious and exotic vacation with Stefano joining me later. A villa on the sea that had been in all the magazines on architecture: it had plants and trees outside and inside the house, a fully equipped gym where I could train, guests of great refinement and a steady stream of jet-setting friends. Brazil is a land with panache and a joy that is unmatched in the world.

On another occasion, when we performed the show *Ladies and Gentlemen*, I decided to keep the entire company busy even when no shows were scheduled. The dancers showed remarkable commitment to their work with me although they could have worked with others during the so-called dead times. This tour that we were going to do touched most of South America, besides Brazil, Peru and Venezuela.

When Franco Felice, one of the dancers, learned that the tour would touch Peru, he persuaded me to go with the rest of the company, during the break between the repeat shows, to visit the archaeological site of Machu Picchu, one of the new seven wonders of the world. This had been his lifelong dream. Although I didn't like the idea of planning a vacation that would loosen the inner tension necessary for such a demanding tour, I was persuaded to agree. Besides what better time could there be, with a week between shows in Lima and the next in Venezuela!

We were advised not to go to straight from Lima to Machu Picchu, 2,400 metres above sea level, without stopping first in Cusco, a city with an altitude of over 3,300 metres. We were told to stay at least a couple of days to acclimatize and avoid altitude sickness. For a dancer to undergo these jumps during a tour is certainly not ideal, which is why Franco decided to give up his dream. But then Claudio Marchetti, another dancer, went on the attack to persuade me to face this adventure.

While in Cusco some illness had already begun to manifest itself. Drinking the *mate de coca* did not help! The first to show signs of discomfort was the promoter himself. As soon as he got off the plane, he took refuge in his room and requested his partner, my assistant choreographer, to go to the pharmacy to look for some medicine. In the days following, almost all the dancers, except me, felt sick. One of the dancers developed a high fever with severe shivering on the train that brought us back from Machu Picchu to Cusco. He literally had to be carried to the hotel.

Apart from these setbacks, I found the location of Machu Picchu created on the highest peak of a mountain, which seems unattainable from below but impressive from above, extraordinary. It is incredible that such a citadel could be built when there were not even helicopters.

I thought everything bad would end there, but the real surprise was in Caracas. The stage of the Ateneo Theatre was enormous, both in depth and in width. To perform *Ladies and Gentlemen*, especially the first part, considerable strength, physical vigour and a lot of breath were required. I noticed immediately, although the audience couldn't, that the dancers seemed a bit strange. I later learned that practically everyone behind the scenes thought they would have a heart attack. They didn't have enough air in their lungs and felt like they were slowing down.

It was in that theatre, on the stage, considered among the hardest in the world, that I collapsed during the last bow of the previous act owing to a damaged meniscus. I returned to Italy in a wheelchair.

Since then I have strictly forbidden any vacation detours during tours. With me you work. That is it!

New Mexico is a land that brings out the mystery of the soul, a psychic spirituality. Through its wide and silent spaces that have all the shades of the warm colours of the earth, it exudes serenity and lightness in an uncomplicated lifestyle, attracting many New Yorkers and others to relocate there.

In Albuquerque and Santa Fé, we presented *Making Dance* after touring London, Hungary, Portugal, Spain and New York. I so loved New Mexico that at the end of each tour I stayed there for weeks with my friends, including Radisha who had moved there from Los Angeles.

We danced in Egypt, Morocco and Senegal. At the Daniel Sorano National Theater in Dakar, Senegal, we hosted a jam session with Senegalese jazzmen and dancers. Giovanni Tommaso played contrabass and electric bass, and Luis Agudo on percussion and birimbao. They played until the morning in the city's Jazz Club.

A well-known local choreographer planned a typical dinner for us. We found ourselves sitting on the floor around a large round table, with a huge plate of rice in the middle, with meat and vegetables around it. We were taught to eat with the hands in their way, with each person marking out his own slice: their good manners consist in not trespassing on the other's wedge!

We danced at the Cairo Opera House, Eygpt, which I was familiar with from one of my first excursions there as a teenager. At the party after the show held in the Ambassador's residence, we found ourselves with all the political and cultural figures of the city. Egyptians and Indians have a freedom and spontaneity typical of ancient cultures that draw spirituality from the heart rather than from the mind.

Canada and Australia are similar in that they both have large spaces. Australia, in particular, is compelling for its wide expanses. The space is infinite with so few inhabitants that it gives the impression that one is living on the moon. In the first tour to debut in Melbourne, all of us behind the scenes thought the theatre was empty because of the total silence in the auditorium. But we were told the show was sold out. That is how the Australians are.

It is one of the farthest countries from Italy and a flight to get there is one of the longest. Because of the jetlag, it was a big challenge to maintain balance while dancing, which as in life, is the key to success and happiness. One of my dancers lost his balance on stage and could not turn this mishap into a creative movement, like a professional must do. It was the first and last time it happened in my show because on stage, I believe that error does not exist and must always be transformed into a dynamic starting point.

The tour continued from Australia to India, on the invitation of Georg Lechner, director of the Goethe-Institut where I had performed at the East-West Dance Encounter event, which he had curated and arranged a year earlier.

During the flight from Sydney to Bombay a distressing news was announced: Indira Gandhi had been assassinated by her bodyguards. The violent destruction of a prominent emblem of a liberal, developing country shocked us all.

We found the airport manned by the army and were immediately escorted to the hotel under the protection of the German host-organizers. India was under curfew and in national mourning for two weeks, with all activities suspended. On that occasion, we had the opportunity to see the greatness of the country. In similar circumstances, the West at most observes a few minutes of silence.

The innate Indian attitude of acceptance was contagious and we too accepted the dramatic events despite our disappointment that all of the shows had to be cancelled. We couldn't find a flight for an early return, so we spent the entire time with some musician friends whose shows had also been cancelled.

A few years later there was another event with India that did not go through. Himachal Som, India's ambassador in Rome, proposed to the Indian government that my company be part of the prestigious Khajuraho Dance Festival, at the site of the famous temples. He appreciated my dance, and I can say with pride, like many Indians. Furthermore, at the invitation of the Indian government, through the ICCR (Indian Council of Cultural Relations), I had already completed a tour of fifteen Indian cities in 1981. The proposal was accepted with enthusiasm. However, there was a problem—the Italian Ambassador refused to support the Indian government's invitation, causing a diplomatic standoff.

It infuriated Himachal Som, despite the fact that the project was part of the cultural exchanges between the two countries. A refusal was unacceptable, considering the years of resounding success I had enjoyed in India. I never did find out the reason behind the refusal. Was it a game of some underhand power or some influential enemy acting against me?

On the occasion of the Seoul Olympics in 1988, we were invited to dance at the Olympics Art Festival by committee members who had seen us perform at the International Dance Festival, a year ago. I was able to see the city's metamorphosis from one year to the next, and observe the Koreans remarkable constructive will as a result of their strong love and commitment to their nation. During our stay, we had two employees of the organization available day and night, always smiling and willing to help.

If only Italians shared this attitude of offering oneself to one's country, Italy would be like a heaven on earth in terms of quality of life.

At this point, I feel compelled to tell you about a bitter episode, the most painful moment of my career, which involved the inclusion of the show *Cleopatra–Il Potere dell'Amore* (Cleopatra–The Power of Love) in the programming of the Teatro dell'Opera di Roma, the opera house in Rome. It was a nerve-racking negotiation with the Superintendent, with pull and push bargaining that made me realize that he expected some sort of under-the-counter transaction, which I would never have agreed to.

In the end, however, the project went through thanks to the fact that my co-producer was Angelo Valori, an influential composer producer and educator, who created the music with his Jazz music ensemble.

By now you know how I respond to different vibrations of people and places. I have rarely perceived as much negativity as in this Italian *carrozzone*, the bandwagon where the energy stems from indifference and carelessness, to the point where it resembles a caricature of the classic Roman proverb loosely translated as "No will to work? Then jump on me!"

I was subjected to presumption, arrogance and misuse of power in every area, as well as complete ineptitude from the press office to the usher. Their negative vibes filled me with fatigue and heaviness. Even my collaborators, unaware of it, started to absorb them, allowing themselves to adopt attitudes they had never had before. I struggled ten times more than usual to get everything in place.

Totally unlike this experience was the performance of *Tosca–Il Potere dell'Amore* (*Tosca–The Power of Love*) in Castel Sant'Angelo, on concession for two consecutive years, by Claudio Strinati, a cultured and refined gentleman, who was superintendent of the Polo Museale Romano. Highly positive vibrations, international audience, magical place and one of the most beautiful castles in the world.

This was the time of impromptu daytime performances, in the form of *happenings*, on the terrace overlooking the city, and in the evenings, reproductions of the entire show in the halls inside. I had the thrill of feeling at one with the character of Tosca and the place. Ioska Mezal, Francesco Tosoni and Max de Bernardini are three young jazz, pop and rock performers who created live music. For the show *Dance To Jazz*, I invited John Arnold, a New York jazz percussionist, to collaborate, and he improvised the music live.

As in *Cleopatra–The Power of Love, Tosca–The Power Against Love* and *Hyde & Eva*, earlier, the word and the story, literally and figuratively had penetrated my choreography in a rather dream-like and surreal way.

In 2015 I choreographed, recited and danced to Anghelos Trojani's poems with no music. When voice and movement merge and become one in sublimating the poetic content, a new synthesis takes place in which one reinforces the other; expressiveness is freed along with greater communicative force.

The audience is interested in understanding poetry since it is visualized in movement. This experience deepened my potential for bringing together the expressiveness of the body with that of the word in harmony with each other.

Reba, the wife of Ambassador Himachal Som, was a friend of mine. A naturally elegant and stylish woman, she is a writer, singer and her scholarship on Tagore is very impressive. After a long stay in Rome, she was posted as the director of the ICCR (Indian Council for Cultural Relations) Kolkata. When I went to India in 2018, she had moved to Delhi and she hosted me at the India International Centre. On that trip, once again, poetry and dance came together for me.

It was providence that I met Sukrita during this sojourn. Sukrita and I were introduced to each other over coffee at the stunning IIC, bordered by the famous Lodhi Gardens, and one of the most culturally vibrant places in the city. At first glance, I felt a deep connection and familiarity with her and she responded in the same way and presented me a volume of her poems. I consider Sukrita a true artist and a beautiful human being.

When I read her poems I was moved by what she had to say and instantly started to visualize movements, just like when I listen to music that speaks to me. I believe that the seeds of our friendship sown at that time, will grow further in the years to come. Her mind comes out of a real synthesis between the Eastern and Western cultures, as does mine.

This is due to her innate sensitivity and I believe that true culture evolves from sensitivity more than anything else. Herself a writer, professor and literatteur, Sukrita also happens to be the daughter of the eminent writer, Joginder Paul.

My forthcoming show *The Dancing Word (Out of the Box)* will be based on poems by Sukrita and Anghelos. I think that music and dance are inherently poetic. As I worked on Sukrita's poems I experienced a new process evolving, quite different from the earlier one.

It involves more than simply immersing oneself in the mystery of words and letting inspiration flow from them in order to produce meaningful movements that will subsequently be expressed through the body. In this instance, it is more important to let the subconscious reverberate with the meaning of the movements so that the other movements—which are limitless and do not wish to be fixed, as I have been doing previously—can arise. I am compelled to trust the calling.

The new approach involves envisioning and imagining movements, observing them as they undergo infinite evolutions, and knowing that they will reappear repeatedly on stage while being further altered during the improvisational process.

I will have to keep the connection with every word of the poem by recreating the same inner state, the right one, the fertile ground, and the openness to inspiration as when the first movements were generated.

However, I will also have to recreate the same state of surrender in which the creative movements, which are in the background, spontaneously emerge. I will need to have faith that I will be ready to invite them to rise again in the act of improvisation.

This procedure is similar to adding live bacteria to milk to create yogurt and then allowing it to multiply, preserving a tiny amount each time to add to more milk to create more yogurt.

What really matters and what will really have to be done is to cultivate the will to keep this process alive. In this sense, one is caught between living in the now and not being held back by the past. The movement is born to die and to give birth to the next one at the same time. While working on Anghelos's poetry, a different kind of creativity came to me which involved matching my voice and pronunciation to a predetermined, specifical choreography.

In Sukrita's poems, each word creates a sense of space and has its own tempo beneath the surface. The combinations of words create a pattern and a rhythm that further elicits a fresh play of movements on the images that have been evoked.

I was asking myself today, *Why, as an artist, it seems simpler for me to fully express my enthusiasm in my work than it is in my interpersonal interactions?* The answer is that, since I am a dreamer, I am able realize my dreams in my art exactly as I am inspired to , while in relationships one must confront the concrete reality of having to interact with the other. While I am able to manage all of my emotional and behavioural excesses in my art, I am not in complete control of my relationships and have to make a lot of compromises.

Actually in both cases, it is like walking on the razor's edge. In an artistic creation, the effort is to let the essence of the inspiration find its own way to be expressed and communicated. The goal in interpersonal interactions is to strike a balance between respecting one's own independence and being tolerant and accepting of the realities of others. These are the qualities which will allow each to give their best.

While speaking with Sukrita about this process, I sat at the Sabaudia's dunes with my feet in the pristine Mediterranean Sea and she in her air-conditioned Delhi home. She stated, "In human relationships one is not alone, there is also the *other*, and it is not easy to deal with what's happening within the other. In art, one is able to freely shape their own creation because they are alone and have greater autonomy over their creative process. However, there is no denying that art too has its own demands, and due respect has to be given to these demands also."

My dream, my aspiration is to get to live my passion in human relationships too, to be able to steer my emotions but also protect myself from the possibility of the other pushing me off my precarious balance. Perhaps the key is to surrender to the other completely while at the same time, remaining conscious of one's own inner world. What will unite the two, possibly integrating them into one, is the capacity to fully see the inner world of the other while simultaneously defending one's own. The two worlds are distinct, yet united. Is this what we call love?

How beautiful it is for us poets to talk about such matters between us! Sukrita and me.

Patrizia Cerroni, Italian dancer, choreographer, director

Patrizia as a six-year-old

Patrizia's parents Bruna
Muzzi and Alfredo Cerroni

Patrizia as a sixteen-year-old

Patrizia with her dance
master Jean Cebron

Guido Paolo Menocci

Guido and Patrizia

Guido's self-portrait

The logo of Patrizia's dance company symbolizing the sun

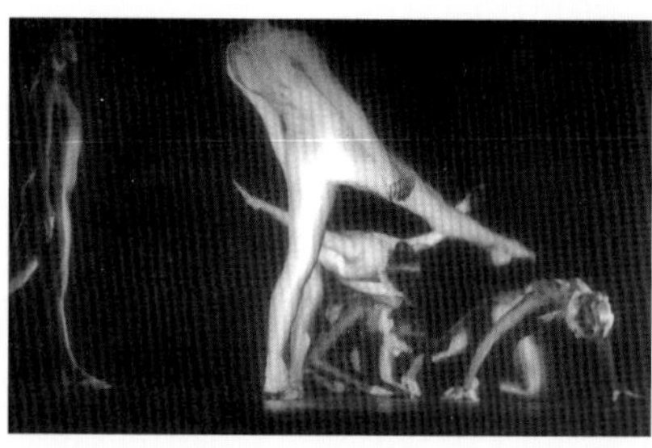

Patrizia Cerroni & Barefoot Dancers in *Hmm ...*, Regio Theatre, Turin, Italy, 1977

Patrizia in *Tendrils ... and my dreams echoed with his melodies*, Kammerspiele, Innsbruck, Austria, 1981

Patrizia at the International
Centre, New Delhi, India, 1983

Patrizia and Luis Agudo in *Concerto*, Elisio
Theatre, Rome, Italy, 1983

Patrizia in *Tendrils ... and my dreams
echoed with his melodies*, Max
Mueller Bhavan, Calcutta, India, 1984

Patrizia at the East-West Dance
Encounter, Tata Theatre, Mumbai,
India, 1984

Barefoot Dancers in *Ladies and Gentlemen*, Olympic Theatre, Rome, Italy. 1988

Patrizia in *Divertissement Lyrique*, Maler Saal, Hamburg, Germany, 1989

Giovanni Tommaso, Patrizia, LuisAgudo in *Concert*, Morlacchi Theatre Umbria Jazz, Perugia, Italy, 1989

Patrizia Cerroni & Barefoot Dancers in *Hyde and Eva*, Olympic Theatre, Rome, Italy, 1995

Patrizia Cerroni & Barefoot Dancers in *Crazy Of Loves*, Gala Italia, New York, USA, 1997

Patrizia and Nazareno Santolamazza in *Ladies & Gentlmen*, Simon Bolivar Theatre, Sao Paulo, Brazil, 1998

Patrizia and Corrado Celestini in
But do you really want to understand something of us women?!! Skiathos Festival, Greece, 2004

Poster of Seoul Olympic Arts Festival

Seoul Plate presented to Patrizia to commemorate the 1988 Seoul Olympics

Poster of *Tosca- The Power Against Love*, Castel Sant Angelo, Rome, 2005

Poster of *Cleopatra-The Power Of Love*, Opera House, Rome, 2008

Silver Plaque awarded to Patrizia by Italian President Carlo
Azeglio Ciampi, Rome, Italy, 2005

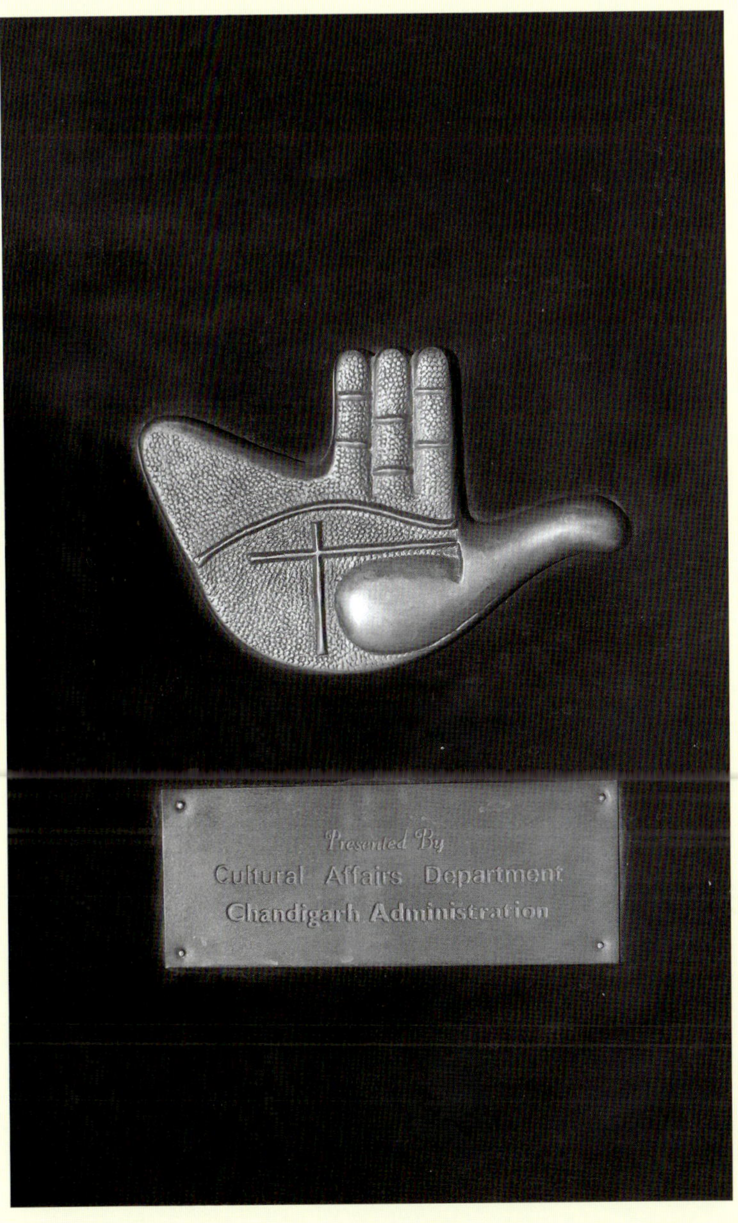

Plaque La Main Ouverte- Le Corbusier awarded to Patrizia by the Indian government, Chandigarh, India, 1981

Patrizia with former Indian ambassador to Italy Himachal Som and his son Vishnu Som, Rome, 1999

Patrizia with Himacha Som and his wife Reba Som, New Delhi, 2019

Sukrita Paul Kumar and Patrizia, New Delhi, 2019

Patrizia and Mario Schifano, Rome, 1997

Patrizia with Chico
Caruso, Rio de Janeiro,
Brazil, 1997

Patrizia Cerroni, Gala Italia, New York, 1995

8

The Planet of Musicians

I was lucky to be the only student enrolled in the Academy's theoretical courses from the fifth to the eighth grade with such teachers as Margherita Abruzzese and Enrico Crispolti for art history, Massimo Coen, the celebrated violinist, for theory of writing music (solfeggio) and Alberto Testa for dance history. I felt like Rousseau's "Eloise" with her tutors.

Mauro Bortolotti, a well-known composer who was a member of Nuova Consonanza, an institution for contemporary music, and a professor of composition at the Conservatory of Rome, was my professor of History of Music. I started studying the history of early twentieth-century music with him. We listened to the compositions and discussed them. Since it was just him and me, we had deep dialogues about art and the inner reality of self, similar to those I later had with Giacinto Scelsi.

Ever since then Mauro and I have developed a relationship just like between two artists rather than between a student and a teacher because he was not the kind of professor who would impart knowledge merely from the chair.

Stravinsky and Schoenberg were the two authors on whom we dwelt the most and who I remember very vividly. We went through John Cage, Luciano Berio, Goffredo Petrassi's electronic music and then Claude Debussy, whose music Jean Cebron was using to create choreographies for us, his students, at the time. Also the musical choice, which led me to create in the Academy the solo *Marche* on Stravinsky's *Histoire du Soldat* when I was eighteen, was inspired by the encounters with Mauro Bortolotti.

After finishing my academic education, I began choreographing to contemporary and electronic music by artists such as Cage, Berio, Stockhausen and Max Neuhaus. My professional association with Mauro began at Beat 72, a temple of the Roman "underground" of those years, during Mauro-themed festival. He invited me to choreograph and dance to *Mottetto*, a piece sung by Michiko Hirayama. Mauro and I performed an improvisation in public for the first time. I was nineteen then.

Mottetto was a solo. As the voice was broken, jerky and sobbing, my movements, were the same. Even in the most dramatic events of my life, I feel a sense of irony. Surely this was the string that Mauro and I shared, through which we were more in tune. When I create choreographies on existing music, my dance miraculously captures every element. This, I believe, is my distinguishing feature; when the music enters inside me, it flows not only into the soul but also into the body, and the body responds, moved by all of its nuances.

For me, this is an instinctively analytical and non-rational process. This is a surrender of the body and soul to music, an experience not accessible to all. This is what happens to the true and naked artists.

Now it was time for Mauro to ask me to compose a choreography on his piece titled *Grazie per essere venuti* (Thanks for Coming), which was intended for solely string instruments. This choreography titled *Concatenazioni* (Concatenations) featured five female dancers.

This was a minimalist choreography based on stillness and linearity of movement, similar to how Mauro's sounds were linear and drawn out. In this particular track of mine, Cunningham's influence is most noticeable particularly in the utilization of space to allow bodies to move freely. While the movements seem to be synchronized randomly, there is an artistic design behind these dynamics of choreography. I believe even in life there is a design even behind coincidences.

Those were artistically intense years. I was a volcano of creativity. I churned out one choreography after another with almost no breaks. I worked in the same way that textbook artists do every day, going to the canvas, the piano and the practice room.

At that time, it was common for choreographers and musicians to create short-lived pieces, developed over time with different motivations, inspirations and music, and then perform them for the public in a single evening. While in India, I started creating unitary shows, which completely changed my way of working. I think I was among the first choreographers in Europe, together with Carolyn Carlson and Pina Bausch, to create monothematic shows.

The first was *Tendrils ... and my dreams echoed with his melodies*. In this show the musicians specially composed the music on my choreography, as would happen later for *C'est ici que l'on prend le bateau* (It's Here Where You Can Take the Boat) a title derived, at Guido's suggestion, from the homonymous poem by Giuseppe Ungaretti written in a visually circular manner.

From 1980, I started using live music. Since I loved rock and pop music, I choreographed on Frank Zappa's music. I recall Mauro arriving at the rehearsals enthusiastic about those pieces, which were scratchy, provocative, grotesque, transgressive and shocking for right-thinking, prim and polite people. He had an open mind, at a time when, as you might expect, contemporary musicians were very closed to rock-pop music. Mauro was literally forced by Guido to appreciate Frank Zappa.

Mauro, sitting or reclining on the cushions in our studio, with headphones on his ears, was bombarded with that music: we "zapped" him.

It was in Babuccio where everything happened; where he met a dear friend of Guido's, Simonetta Lux, who often joined us in our evenings, our memorable parties, and with whom Mauro had a long and intense love story. For *Tendrils*, I turned to jazz, for *C'est ici que l'on prend le bateau* I commissioned the music from Mauro. I created the latter as a four-hour show and choreographed it in Italy after returning from India.

These two shows followed the same procedure, almost like a twin birth: they were different from each other, yet linked from the moment of conception. When I returned to Italy from India, after finishing *Tendrils*, and touring it throughout Europe, I began working on *C'est ici ...* When the tour of *Tendrils* ended, I started the rehearsals of *C'est ici...*, which lasted three months. *C'est ici ...* premiered at the Kamani Auditorium, Delhi, in February 1981.

For Mauro as for all the members of the company, India was an experience that left an indelible mark. The tour lasted three weeks. We were nine dancers, Mauro, two technicians for sound and light, and the photographer Sebastiana Papa. The ICCR (Indian Council for Cultural Relations) had organized the tour. We presented the show in the fifteen major cities across India, in the largest theatres, for a total of seventeen performances.

While in *Tendrils*, the choreographies and movements of the bodies evolved like Indian music and jazz improvising on the theme, while in *C'est ici que l'on prend le bateau*, I choreographed the movements by fixing them in each step, allowing only few flashes of improvisation in the second half of the show.

Mauro came daily to the rehearsals, observed the choreographies in silence and then we analyzed them in detail later. After having conveyed to him the kind of sonority I wanted, he made notes and more notes, timing all the passages of the movements to meet my request that he should express every movement perfectly with his music. They were notes that turned into electronic music, which he recorded on tape; after hearing them together, we agreed on the latest nuances and continued.

I have a secret to reveal to you: I often created the rhythmical elements of the show inspired by Bob Marley's music on which I liked to improvise, as well as David Bowie's music on which I wanted to create the most airy and harmonious dynamics.

The first half of the show was based on recorded electronic music on which he improvised live on stage with the synthesizer, while in the second half he focused on dance-inspired improvisations on the piano. It was a huge amount of work, and one day he told me, "I have never worked so hard in my life!" It was a continuous back and forth, but like me, he too was pleased with the result.

Our show was a huge success. Until then, I don't think that kind of music had ever been played live in India. A press conference was held in Delhi to interview me, with over fifty journalists from all states attending. My photo was published on the front page of *The Hindustan Times*, holding a cigarette, because I was smoking at the time. It was unusual for the Indian government to invest in international artists in this way, and I was extraordinarily amazed and flattered. It felt like there was a divine plan behind it.

I accompanied Mauro to the Theosophical Society, Madras, where I was moved by the sight of a thousand-year-old banyan tree. I remember Mauro sitting with me on the bench, contemplating the tree that looked like a forest, with branches intertwined and rooted in the ground around the main trunk. Under that tree 500 people could have taken shelter. Tears welled up in his eyes as he spoke about his father. India is the land where tears seem to wash away the suffering of the world, like the waters of a river that comes from far away.

Unfortunately, I gradually reduced the duration of *C'est ici …* committing a grave error, that I may still be perpetuating in all of my works today: I put only the essential on stage, much to the surprise of my dancers who, after hours of highly elaborate and functional choreography, see a maximum of ninety minutes presented on stage.

Even with this book you are reading, I tried to do the same, but then I stopped because I realized that its strength is precisely in the emotional dimension that cannot pass through a sieve of a rational composition that would deplete it of its quality, even if it would help to better understand the difficult passages for those who live exclusively in that dimension of the mind that tends to suffocate their emotions. In the case of *C'est ici*, the choreography lost its cosmic space-time sense, which went beyond the sense of real time.

After a sort of preview in Pavia to run the show ahead of the tour in India, the hours went to three, after India from three to two and, during the tours in Europe, we arrived at one hour, with Mauro obviously cutting the music step by step.

"*C'est ici...*" was an intense journey, and whenever there is an opportunity I will put it back to its original length. I consider it a universal, monumental, choral work, and its power is precisely in its outstretched temporal extension. The space-time Jungian synchronicity is visually realized. It puts the movement in relation with the cosmos and the infinite, the load-bearing elements—those elements that sustain our lives. Like infinity, dance has a great linearity of movement that extends beyond itself; like the cosmos, it has circular dynamics, similar to those of planets or flocks of birds.

As in *Concatenations* so also in *C'est ici ...*, Cunningham and his influence in the use of space is evident. The work also contains a minimalist and essential element, a gestural dimension inspired by concrete life. Here my dance begins to express in a more accentuated way the ambivalence between abstraction and realism. It is my only work where there is no trace of paradoxes because they are not necessary. This show lives in another dimension, mystical and spiritual.

C'est ici ... and *Tendrils* were featured in the programme schedule for two weeks at the Teatro Eliseo in Rome where dance had never been previously performed, and the tickets were all sold out. The hall was always full. We also drew full houses at the Teatro Olimpico, Rome. I am a person and an artist who has never sought connections in the structures that govern and administer dance in Italy, yet I had enjoyed the widespread appreciation of critics and the general public in many countries around the world especially Europe.

I enjoyed excellent relationships in the world of music and theatre, and so I frequently featured in musical and theatrical programming. Mauro Bortolotti introduced me to Franco Evangelisti, a prominent figure in the field of music, who immediately invited me and my company to participate in a festival of newly improvised contemporary music by an influential avant-garde music group Nuova Consonanza of which Franco was the president.

In the following years, I collaborated with Mauro again and composed the music for *Divertissement Lyrique*, a women-only show with six female dancers and live instrumental music performed with a bow, a cello, a viola and Mauro at the piano on the stage.

On the occasion of its debut at the Teatro Olimpico it so happened that Diego Gullo, president of the theatre of Rome at that time, liked the show very much and invited me to perform at the Argentina theatre a month later, provided I brought a new show. When I distraughtly mentioned it to Vittoria Ottolenghi, a well-known dance critic, that I had so little time, she immediately told me: "Change the music and the costumes and present the same show with a new title."

For the first time, I followed her suggestion and renamed it *Concerto*. I contacted Giovanni Tommaso and Luis Agudo, transformed some choreographic passages and proposed the same show "in disguise". It worked so well that I eventually stopped listening to Mauro's instrumental music and instead started preferring jazz. This was between 1985 and 1986.

Mauro was not disappointed; we had a fantastic understanding between us, and we loved each other. He was a beautiful person, ironic, intelligent, human, simple and humble. We remained friends and he continued to support me until his untimely death in 2007.

Giacinto Scelsi is widely acclaimed as one of the greatest musicians of our time. His music is imposing, echoing the power of the cosmos to the point of becoming omnipotent, capable of expressing the emptiness of darkness and light, to the point of making the listener feel the experience of all the emotions, including fear. Hearing his music makes you happy.

Michiko Hirayama, a Japanese singer and important interpreter of contemporary music, introduced me to Scelsi. Both Mauro and Giacinto had created pieces dedicated to her voice. With Michiko, we started a collaboration based on experimental improvisations that turned out to be stimulating and fun. We brought them on stage and were much appreciated by Antonioni when he came to attend one of our performances.

Musicians relate to me as if I were a musician who creates and inspires sound with movement that they do not hear but see. We create together; the sound does not interfere with the movement in the physical space, since the music does not constitute another body, just as the movement does not overlap with the sound, as would happen with another musician. We are exclusively a stimulus for one another that does not create interference but leaves the relationship free. This occurs during improvisation between any style of dance and music. Dance and music constantly come together in a great interplay.

Michiko and I undoubtedly struck up an instant rapport because she was Oriental, but also because she was under the master tutor Giacinto Scelsi, whom I had yet to meet. Michiko's value in my life is that thanks to her I met him. At that time, Giacinto was a "burnished" wise old man, and I was a "reckless" wise young woman.

I believe the first meeting says everything, including the potential that exists between two people. It was a love of artists at first sight! Our bond was immediately intense, and like all true friendships would last forever. I met him in 1980 when I returned from my first trip to India, and we had a daily exchange until his disappearance in 1988.

To me, he was a very special person with his large, ecstatic blue eyes that led straight into the infinite. Giacinto seemed to live in a state of equipoise spreading peace all around him. Calibrated in every gesture and word, he was always willing to listen to the other, and while he was curious, he was highly selective about the topics.

He explained to me what was happening in me as I created and danced, and in this way helped me to understand it. Before meeting him, I was not fully conscious of the creative process, despite the fact that I was continuously expressing it.

He once he told me, "The artist *finds*, does not *look for*". I believe he meant that the one who seeks, or looks for, but does not find is a mere experimenter. A true artist is more than that.

Giacinto Scelsi has been to me a master and philosopher, who has contributed greatly to my understanding of how an artist is a channel for the flow of divine inspiration. This approach, in my opinion, applies not only to artists, but to everybody who, at any time, in any act of life, wishes to establish the ideal conditions to activate this same power.

I often improvised for him on silence in his magical house overlooking the Palatine Hill. As a choreographer, I decided to go back to other musical genres I was always passionate about, such as jazz, Indian music, rock, pop, new age. Although I had moved away from contemporary music, he came to all my shows, respected and followed my creative evolution, regardless of the musical genres I chose at the time.

We talked about our experience as artists, his as a composer and mine as a choreographer. It was a continuous and infinite dialogue; two artists like us can spend eternity exploring these themes because they are our breath, our water, our daily bread. He explained to me how we were both "spikes" able to open new gateways and how, for this reason, when we reached the summit, we were alone and we had to accept solitude. He added that we didn't feel "alone" because in fulfilling our mission with devotion we gave humanity the benefits of our efforts.

When one comes back to earth, one is happy to share with others one's experiences and creations. I believe that God speaks to us only when it is necessary to guide us in fulfilling our purpose; for the rest of the time, he leaves us to understand the message, to then be ready to listen to it again.

That was a time when I was extremely productive. I would create a new theme on which to develop movement, and then run to show it to him. He was happy about it and by participating in its creation he encouraged me, helping me to understand the sense and value of what I had created, with his in-depth analysis and comments that inspired me to move forward.

He told me about his life in Paris and his relationship with Romans. He too, like me, suffered from the provincialism of our country, we both knew we were "white flies", as we say in Italian to describe special and unusual people, in a restricted and envious milieu that was not able to recognize and appreciate our true value.

Giacinto did not feel understood as he would be in the future. He encouraged me to become aware of this problem, that I too would have to learn to be tough. According to him, we were kindred souls. He told me that I was the only artist he had ever met who was like him. He prepared me to be strong and to understand what I had already undergone. In this way, he helped me protect myself from pain which, as a misunderstood artist he knew well, and, unlike me, he had already achieved detachment.

He used to tell me, "It is normal and inevitable that others will misunderstand you and envy you. You keep going without worrying because such valuable art will continue to exist. You will be considered inconvenient by those who will have power because your role is to be their conscience. Prepare yourself because you will be crucified and tortured." Giacinto was a great help and support during difficult times because he understood how I felt. He provided me moral support and encouraged me to move ahead.

He once told me that in the Italian musical scene, Franco Evangelisti was his only friend (!!!!), a true artist who understood his music. Franco is no longer among us but he lives on through the Isabella Sclesi Foundation.

The positive aspect of the difficulties we artists have to go through is that they awaken in us the original and mysterious power of life. If those crucifixions and tortures are overcome, nothing can be frightening anymore, anything can be accomplished, even flying.

The artist confines himself in his atelier till life forces him to leave the shell and the cave to interact with the outside world. He must follow a path that is viable, in which to deal with reality.

Giacinto provided me with immense support, just as Guido had done. They knew each other and respected each other. Giacinto did not step out easily from his small building in Via di San Teodoro, above the Roman Forum and in front of the Palatine Hill, but he made an exception for us and visited us a few times at Babuccio. Whenever we visited him, he welcomed us warmly. In his house, there was a constant flow of visitors from all over the world—French musicians, philosophers and poets, American models, an ensemble that embraced every field of international social and cultural life.

Once I even met Allen Ginsberg in one of the parties held in his honour at Giacinto's apartment. He told me that his house was located in a part of Rome that served as an esoteric nexus of interchange between the energy of the East and the West. Both Giacinto at his palace and myself with Guido at Babuccio organized wonderful parties and created meeting points for artists.

In the summer, just the two of us went to his terrace to soak in the sun during the warmest hours, and I was naked because I felt entirely comfortable with him. We shared a fondness for the sun and the heat so we were similar in this regard. A real madness! I could talk to him about my private life there in the sun, but he would always cut me short and say, "An artist like you cannot have a life of normal relationships".

Giacinto believed that my art and I were outside the bounds of normality, so he thought I couldn't and shouldn't have a love life. Marcello Carosi said the same to me, but I never accepted their point of view. Even though I am an artist, with a rather complex temperament, I believe that it could be difficult but not impossible to create a union of love that could be my masterpiece.

Giacinto denied that this was possible because he was unable to bring his genius and power into human love. It is the artist's dilemma; an artist can only satisfy his desire to love through the creative act due to his extreme humanity. He is afraid of suffering in love, so he escapes into art. Risking love relationships has been a fantastic enrichment for me, which I bring to my dance as well.

In this regard, I want to tell you about an old movie, *The Red Shoes*, which I saw as a child. The film tells the story of a dancer who falls madly in love with a man while rehearsing for a big debut. The manager forces her to choose between dance and love because, in his vision, the two things cannot coexist. Torn, she chooses to continue dancing and gives up love, remaining unhappy all her life. This perception was, perhaps still is, quite powerful in the world of art. I have never been convinced of that, even though, as you know, *a la manièr de moi*, in my own way, I found myself subscribing to it.

Today, I feel compelled to tell you that it is the exact opposite. Any form of art necessitates the capacity for absolute love, beyond the narrow confines of romantic human love; nevertheless, if the artist is able to love his partner in the same "absolute", it would do nothing but fuel energy, multiplying it a hundredfold. I always thought that dance was a sort of a tyrant but in the good sense that I just showed you. Everything is relative because it depends on how you live it.

Giacinto and I had a frank and free-flowing talk on this subject and the artist's creative process. In my opinion, the artist descends into the mystery of human existence, captures the root and then sublimates it through symbol and sign; for Giacinto, the artist only receives inspiration from above. In my experience the miracle occurs when the inspiration from above reaches the depths of being in which the very roots of that inspiration reside, recreating the connection between the high and the deep.

That was the time when I began my journey in psychoanalysis. It was Giacinto who suggested that I contact a Jungian psychotherapist when I told him that I needed to deepen my understanding of my dreams. I had been having a lot of dreams for a long time.

When I told Giacinto about my experiences in psychotherapy, he changed the subject. He didn't want to hear about it. He said that the only way to remove the darkness in the cellars was to bring light from above. In my opinion, it is necessary to go into the unconscious to purify it with the appropriate therapeutic tools. Like many artists, he believed that art could serve as a spiritual tool for solving the most profound human issues. Music was his tool for transcending and resolving his conflict with life. For me, dance is the instrument that allows me to transcend reality. I believe self-care has to happen through a different process, namely therapy.

Although Giacinto didn't usually want his music to be choreographed as an exception he asked me to do it. One day, he gave me the original tape of one of his improvisations from which his masterpiece, *Ko-Tha* (Dance of Shiva) was born. In this piece, he laid the guitar flat as if it were a percussion. He asked me to choreograph it, I remember his exact words: "You are the only one who can interpret the Dance of Shiva."

At that time, I didn't feel like choreographing his music, which was magnificent. He understood that I was on other musical waves at the time, having just come off ten years of being immersed in modern music, but he told me with tremendous certainty that one day I would dance it. And so it was.

In 2005, through Gisella Belgeri, I met Nicola Sani, director of the Scelsi Foundation, who invited me to interpret the Dance of Shiva at the Scelsi Festival, completely unaware that Giacinto had requested the same twenty-five years earlier. This was simply fate, and Giacinto had foreseen the future! On that occasion I presented the Scelsi Foundation the original recording of *Ko-Tha*, which I had kept for all those years as a sacred and precious gift, and which we revived to commemorate Giacinto's birth centenary.

We performed the choreography on *Ko-Tha* at the Goethe-Institut in Rome, with live musical performance by percussionist Antonio Caggiano. On that occasion, I was able to share with him the explanations that Giacinto had given me, many years before, about the meanings of the sounds and the profound significance of that piece.

Dance and music allow people to see and hear God. In the choreography I dedicated to Giacinto, the austere initial sounds and movements appear to indicate the first steps of Lord Shiva in the world, unleashed in rhythms and dynamics in a gradual crescendo. Giacinto is an immensely great artist.

His value was not recognized until much later, and he began to reap the benefits of his art only in the last years of his life. He, like many other artists, is getting full recognition only after his death, in this country of ours. As with Cunningham, I felt that I was in the right place, at the right time with the right person. This is what is happiness!

I spoke extensively about Giacinto Scelsi because he was a genius, a genuine artist, a great human being and divine, most dear and important to me. He left a lasting impression on me and shaped the course and direction of my life.

Giacinto, you are in excellent company with Guido, Jean Cebron, Merce Cunningham, Marcello Carosi, Fabio Mauri, David Zard, Antonio Negro, Dino Orlando.

Thank you all for all you have given me!

Thank you for becoming the ideal representation of all of your values and having transmitted them to me with generosity and affection. I feel like I am each of you. Let this book captivate you with the same power that I have received from you all, and may it benefit all who read it.

Another important musician in my life was the tabla maestro Zakir Hussain.

The first time I saw him in Delhi he was twenty-eight years old; I was really impressed by the way he played the tabla—it was as if the tabla were talking. He communicated through tabla and his music was lyrical, dramatic, at times comical as well as serious. He transmitted all human emotions through the tabla, lifting the listener to a higher dimension. I realized that as artists both of us had the same way of perceiving and approaching life.

I choreographed on two of his albums, *Making Music* and *Space*. I created *Making Dance* on *Making Music* and *Ali in corpo* (Wings in the body) on *Space*. When Zakir's sister, Khurshid, came to see *Making Dance* in London, she told me that she had never seen anyone express all of the complexities and emotions found in Indian music through body dynamics in this way. I have travelled the world with both of these shows.

In *Making Music*, two Western musicians and two Indian musicians improvise together: Hariprasad Chaurasia on flute, Zakir on tabla, John McLaughlin on guitar and Jan Garbarek on saxophone. This musical composition allows you to recognize the Indianness in a Western dimension and in dance, the Western as reflected in the oriental dimension. In *Making Dance*, each dancer moves along one of the instruments, capturing every musical passage.

The choreography is created by the four dancers' interpretations, with everyone dancing rigorously solely on his particular instrument. At supper following the concert in Rome, John McLaughlin expressed regret that he had not had an interaction like Zakir had with me.

In *Space*, Zakir achieves that same East-West synthesis that I realize in the show *Ali in Corpo*. In the first half of the piece, the choreography, influenced by electronic music, creates movements resembling a flock of birds, which intersect and expand into groups that take abstract forms in the space defined in various shades of light blue by the stage lighting.

The second part, on a magical piece of minimalist percussion, the dancers in red bodysuits, with bare arms and legs, play rhythmically with each other, with broken, delicate and ironic movements, to which they add scatts, creating an imaginary language in a meaningless but very expressive nonsense conversation.

The encounter with Indian music opened me to understanding, even before I met Giacinto Scelsi, how my dance had the same element as the flow of a river. The smooth movement symbolically expresses the deepest emotions which are connected to the divine within the human being.

Indian dance is dynamic in its gestures, facial expressions, footwork rhythms and in the curves of the body, but it does not move into space dynamically as Indian music does. One aspect of this music is similar to the way my dance language flows in space.

Zakir, like me, lived between America and India. Over the years our paths had crossed at different places around the world, and every time I see the affinity of the path that our souls are on, and I recognize his evolution was similar to mine.

He introduced me to Georg Lechner, the director of the Goethe-Institut in Mumbai, who hosted me for four months in his house overlooking the Indian Ocean. His Korean wife and I also studied German together. I was preparing to perform as a guest star in the international festival he curated, *East-West Dance Encounter* at the Tata Theatre in Mumbai, with guests from all over the world including Susan Link from the Folkwang Hochschule (Folkwang Academy).

Georg was a man of great charm, culture and insight. He had been the husband of Sonal Mansingh, the noted Odissi and Bharatanatyam dancer. He had a son, a dancer in Friedman's German company, so he was very sensitive to the madness of artists. He was really fond of me, and became a cautious interlocutor on the challenges and tensions that I was experiencing in my relationship with my Indian twin soul, about which I will tell you later. Georg affectionately told me, after my debut in the festival, that I was not a star but a sun, which in any case is a star.

At that time I was on a tour of Maharashtra with the music legends Zakir Hussain, Hari Prasad Chaurasia, Shiv Kumar Sharma, Brij Bhushan Kabra, V. G. Jog and Vijay Kichlu. I was the lone Western guest and above all the only dancer among them. It was a privilege and an honour for me to participate on their tour. All of them are true artists, people of remarkable simplicity, humility, humanity and integrity. There was great understanding and friendship between us.

We travelled in a bus where the seats had been removed and replaced with a soft carpet that was elegantly and comfortably enriched with mattresses, blankets and silk pillows. There was so much joy, happiness and laughter, but alas, my meniscus gave way and sprang out in each city, blocking my knee. Each time the best orthopaedician was called to reinsert the cartilage that had come out of the joint. Everyone was amazed that I was not able to do it by myself, but I am no Rambo! I would never be able to manipulate the tibia and the femur for that purpose.

The pain that I actually felt was not so much the physical one related to the meniscus, but rather the internal one for the state of conflict that I was experiencing with my soulmate at the time. I was torn between the desire to love him and the fear of doing so, which led me to challenge him, provoke him, and express my distrust in an exasperating and dramatic push and pull. India brings out the best and the worst in one's self. I found myself confronting my existential knot, which I had begun to perceive quite clearly.

My soulmate did not understand the gravity of the problem that I was projecting on him at that moment; he only felt wounded, profoundly rejected and hurt. I hope that on the other side of the coin, which is always present in every manifestation of life, everything that has happened between us may have been useful to him as it was to me, which contributed to my beneficial transformation where necessary. I have changed thanks to him.

In Calcutta, 1984 or thereabouts, I took part in the Classic International Music Festival at Max Mueller Bhavan, where I danced improvising for forty-five minutes in silence with the musicians in the front row "listening" to my silent music. Such an experience was possible only in Calcutta, a city that pulsates with art and culture, and home to one of India's most renowned musical traditions. People even stopped me on the street to pay compliments for that performance, which seemed to have made history.

Chaurasia, the greatest flautist in India, when he saw me dance said, "You are God gifted." It is true that the artist receives a gift from God; she is born with talent.

As you may recall, Guido had passed on his passion for jazz music to me, and he had an impressive collection, from classics to contemporary jazz. Jazz, like rock and pop, had already woven its way into the fabric of my exclusive relationship with contemporary music.

When still a teenager, I went to a Charlie Mingus concert in Todi. I was under the stage, spellbound, watching him play: a powerful body emanating an equally powerful energy, he was one with his double-bass, which he seemed to play with passion while embracing it like it was his lady. From his intense, dazzling and benevolent face, a complicit and sardonic wink was dedicated at me. I smiled shyly, but I was sure both of us were captivated by each other. The double-bass is one of my favourite instruments because it touches deep chords in the belly, where the unconscious resides.

In one of my extended visits in New York I met Susan, Mingus's wife, who was his polar opposite in both personality and appearance. Well, opposites attract after all! We stayed in his apartment, which had an extraordinary view of Manhattan, and stayed up until dawn talking about Mingus. I was very struck when I heard that it was Mingus's desire to have his ashes scattered in the Ganges. Until then, I had not been aware of his love for India.

Years later, in Susan's book, *Around Midnight*, I found many of their love stories which Susan had told me on that night in New York.

I had earlier read the autobiography of Mingus, which, like that of Nijinsky, was short, concise, without punctuation. Even before reading it, I imagined that one day I would write the story of my life in one breath, without commas and full stops but, as you can see, that was not to be. Is it possible that the emotional flow that could transcend the mental dimension has been lost as a result of the way I write it?

Certainly, this approach it is more rational and accessible to all. I don't believe I have betrayed my original intuition; the content of the heart remains the same— dance, music and life—all of which are simply the soul's history.

Mingus's music penetrates and flows in the blood, making every cell of my being echo and shine, intensifying my energy that erupts in strong and erotic movements, rich in complex dynamics and fluid sinuousness, involving all my body from hair to feet. I dance even better on Mingus's music than on "silence", my favourite music. He is *the best!* For me.

I choreographed his song "Percussion Discussion", of which they wrote at the Taormina Arte Festival: "An authentic prima ballerina, not inferior to certain *etoiles* of international dance; Cerroni unleashes herself like a force of nature". The success was due to Mingus. It was a piece that I bravely combined with contemporary music and with Frank Zappa's compositions in the repertoires presented to the public.

After my debut in jazz, I created, on a piece by Sem Rivers, a happening based exclusively on a solid structure of movement themes, on which the dancers improvised. As I have mentioned earlier, *Tendrils* marked the first time I invited jazz musicians to compose original live music for the choreographies.

It was then that I made the decisive transition from contemporary music to jazz, collaborating for many years with Giovanni Tommaso, Luis Agudo, Fulvio Maras, Ettore Fioravanti and Massimo Urbani.

I have an exclusive relationship with jazz music because my dance is inspired by an emotional urge that creates the theme of movement on which the entire performance is built. Fidelity to the theme determines the strength and quality of the composition; this strengthens the theme, which is the pivot of dance, the point of reference, the anchor. With fidelity, you can give your best by deepening and capturing the mystery hidden in the theme itself. Just like a couple's love.

During the European tour of *Tendrils*, with Giovanni Tommaso and Luis Agudo we were able to develop an almost natural relationship of complicity and intimacy between us; it was an exchange of impulses and ideas that bounced and chased each other, between sounds and movements that always seemed to be born in unison. We were travelling on a Ford Transit through the main cities of Austria, Germany, Denmark and Sweden.

We shared everything, spending entire days laughing and joking, talking about our lives and commenting on our emotions on stage. On some occasions, Massimo Urbani joined us with his magical sax and the American singer Joanne Logue. At other times, Luis was replaced by percussionist Fulvio Maras, or Ettore Fioravanti, a drummer. Throughout the tour, Guido was with us charging, spoiling and protecting us, including the lighting and sound technicians who were part of the same beautiful family.

We were always sold out in every city, and in Hamburg, there was a line of a thousand people outside the theatre, forcing us to perform again the next day, unscheduled.

Robert Lindgren, the director of the Dance Department of the University of North Carolina, saw *Concerto* in Rome, and invited us to perform in the theatre of the dance department in Winston-Salem, North Carolina.

According to Robert, Jim Shertzer, one of America's most feared critics, who loved to crush any choreographer, including Cunningham, would have been ruthless with me too. He was thus preparing me for a possibly nasty review. But after Shertzer attended the show in Winston-Salem, he wrote an appreciative article, where he recognized the originality of my dance language, especially when compared to American modern dance. The headline of the article was "It is difficult not to get captivated by the feast of the dynamics of dancers at the Art School". *Concerto* was much loved in the United States. In the following years, I used a third method to link my choreographies to music.

For two of my productions, *Ladies & Gentleman* and *Hyde & Eva*, we created a musical collage of different authors, selected by expert music consultants, Claudio Marchetti, a dancer of my company, and one of his dear friends Danilo Ritucci, who had a music store in Rome.

Claudio was an interpreter of great class and personality, whose energy I absolutely loved and also greatly admired the qualities of his dynamics. He could use his sensitivity and musical culture to choose tracks that would precisely match the atmosphere of the performances. He realized his passion and love for music through dance, which is in fact music played with the body. On the choreographies I created in the silence, step by step they suggested the music. Among the chosen musicians were L Shankar of the Shakti group, Brian Eno, Ashra, Steve Roch and Prince.

I have choreographed many musical genres of various ages (periods) and styles. I believe that dance and music interact in a way that helps them derive raw mutual enrichment. The union of these twin arts is the closest to the realization of androgyny, of which I will write more in detail shortly.

9

My India

The early twentieth-century philosopher and mystic Rudolf Steiner states that every seven years in one's life comes a turning point and that at the age of twenty-eight one connects with one's spiritual roots. The events of that year will reveal their links to one's spiritual evolution and will remain so for the rest of one's life. At that stage in my life, grand India was waiting for me.

I have always felt an existential call for that land. When I was very little and I used to cry by myself and imagine going to a magical land in the East for which I did not yet have a name, where I would find happiness.

And so it was.

I spent an entire year getting ready for the journey. I was often at dinner with Sebastiana Papa, photographer, writer, scholar and expert on India, particularly Indian dance, on which she had written books. She was an extraordinary cook and had written cookery books as well.

Her stories and knowledge of that country served as a prelude for me. India is not a place one goes to unprepared.

I was going through a phase of extreme dissatisfaction at that time. There was too much dance. I needed something else, I needed to find myself in another dimension. Although this was clear to me, I didn't think I could immerse myself in "that" dimension.

Stepping out of the plane, I sensed that dimension—spirituality. It was so tangible and dense, it could be cut with a knife. What an extraordinary place—where love and respect transcend life and death, happiness and sadness, poverty and prosperity. All the extremes overwhelming, but in the lightness of harmony in disharmony. Ironically, in India is where I first started remembering my dreams and where real life seemed more like a dream than reality. For the first time, I had made tangible and palpable contact with my oneiric dimension. I was given the power of dream recall and direct access to my unconscious mind in addition to the gift of the awakening of spiritual energy. Our inner world is intuitive, immense, immeasurable, considerably richer than the concrete and rational one. At that point, I was able to recognize the unconscious dynamics that create the symbols and signs in dreams, so as to actually see them.

A proverb tells us that he who sleeps, does not catch fish, but in my case I can say that it was the exact opposite—the most precious fish I caught was while I was in sleep. Dreaming is my favourite spiritual practice. More than the one I am telling you about, my oneiric existence has been incredibly transcendental. It has been full of adventures, emotions, sensations, understandings, sharing and even a lot of dance the best I have ever done. The dream surpasses reality, it is far from the eyes and goes beyond the heart.

One Indian master once informed me that this one life of mine would be worth ten lives. For over thirty years, I have had a really intense Hollywoodian and Bollywoodian dream production. I had spent at least an hour every morning writing down my dreams, especially during my Jungian journey. My dreams, which I brought out daily like new bread, were preserved by my psychotherapist. In psychotherapy, it is customary to give the patient back all of their dreams at the conclusion of the therapy. In my case it didn't happen because the doctor lost them during a move.

Only one of these visions survived because Luigi Maria Musatti, the director of the Academy of Dramatic Arts "Silvio D'Amico", wanted to incorporate it into the script for *Hyde & Eva*, which we were writing "four-handedly" but ultimately did not use. The script attempted to control the creative flow in a too logical way, while the show had to follow its own irrational wave.

In the dream, I see my back from the waist up in front of a desert with sand dunes that stand out against a clear blue sky under the golden light of a midday sun. I swing, from side to side in slow motion, the long light brown hair, with many shades of honey swaying with me, when a lock of my hair turns into a silvery snake. It slips away, I turn around and chase it for fun.

I am about to catch it but it has become an elusive fish, which flashes out of my hands three times; when I finally manage to grab it, I see with sadness that it gasps for air. I pull out of its mouth a stiff pearl-gray ribbon and handed it to Guido, standing next to me, wailing, "Look, it is dying!"

"It is not dying," he assures me, writing with the ribbon on his palm, "look it leaves its mark!"

In the Christian catacombs of ancient Rome, the symbol of the fish represents Christ. Each sign in astrology is associated with a certain part of the body. For example, the fish, the most spiritual of the zodiac signs, is associated with the feet. In my view, the snake is a symbol of vital energy while the ribbon represents the libido.

The fish is the symbol of identification with the self. In the dream I chase the fish, my self-realization, with the joy of my creative energy in the game, but when I finally grab it, I am afraid. The fish in my hand is gasping, it is dying. I am afraid of death. Thanks to the support of the "other", my friend, I conquer fear. Guido was important to me, his reassuring presence helped me overcome all the difficult challenges of my life.

I invite you to write down your dreams. By doing so, you train yourself to memorize them. The details emerge naturally. Writing down the impressions and thoughts that dreams evoke in us as well as the feelings we experience while dreaming can be helpful in observing and understanding our emotions so that we can live in a better way and avoid pain and suffering. In this way suffering can become a tool for personal development; else, it can destroy one.

"We are such stuff as dreams are made on" — *The Tempest*, William Shakespeare

One of the best things in life was being able to access my unconscious at all times. I have always internalized everything since I was a child. It makes emotions, sensations, thoughts vibrate inside me. I listen to them, and understand them to the point that they become one with me. This process allows me to share my inner world with others, and they freely vibrate even outside of me.

There is no longer any distinction between the internal and external world. What I have inside is perfectly manifested and realized in the external world—this is union. For me, this means to be oneself. What we experience vibrates in us and reconnects us to the original source of everything, which is the divine hidden in our profound mystery, from which everything comes and to which everything returns. The split between internal and external can lead one to act against one's will and desire, creating a rift.

In India, I kept receiving signals that corresponded with what I wanted. I woke up earlier than usual one morning in Madras, determined to get a handbag of black beads. I was taken aback by my rather strange fantasy, which most definitely did not match my taste.

I decided to go and sit on the beach to contemplate on it. In the distance I noticed an Indian woman in a sari, with children playing around her, walking gracefully in my direction. I have always been enchanted by the grace with which Indian women move, they look like queens. I realized that she was coming straight to me. Smiling, with a sweet expression on her face, she gave me a gift—a purse of black beads. Ever since that seemingly little incident, my life has been filled with manifestations that align with my inner wishes.

As I told you earlier, my first trip to India changed the course of my life, transformed me as a person, as a woman and as an artist. It has been a turning point for my art as well. Before going to India, I expressed sorrow, neurosis, contradiction, conflict, incommunicability, loneliness as was done in most Western contemporary art.

My life consisted of dancing and creating, not in a sane way but in a very self-destructive way. It was a highly neurotic way of living for me as it was for many contemporary artists of the 70s. It was a choice we had made by our own will; and we were complicit in it.

We revelled in our neurosis, it was part of a cultural attitude, and we expressed it in an intense way. The art of that period—theatre, music, cinema, painting—was all about breaking canons, destroying existing systems, but flagellating ourselves in the process. I belonged fully to that trend.

My first trip to India was on my own, a solitary path. I took India inside myself, it was in my DNA: it is intense and fundamental. It was a karmic need, like many other artists had—the Beatles, Cunningham, Graham, Terzani.

I travelled to India because I was experiencing a profound existential malaise. I felt a deep yearning to find the meaning of life and God.

I will now explain to you why I was drawn to India and how my spiritual journey began.

It was a mythical, mystical journey.

I must find myself, I can't take this anymore, I am leaving and I don't know how and when I'll be back, I told myself.

All my trips to India lasted about six months, but the first one was the most important. Everything was rekindled; not only did I get very powerful "mythological" dreams, but I had a revival in dance though I had left Italy to detach myself and take a break from it. I felt such a powerful inspiration that I could create two twin shows simultaneously. In addition to the strong reactivation of my creativity, I had magical encounters with the greatest musicians of India, who were the Bach, Beethoven and Mozart of India. They are very important for me as they loved me and immediately recognized me as their equal.

In listening to Indian music, which I believe to be one of the most spiritual in the world, I became those ragas that flowed through my blood.

I danced to that music in a new way, different from the Indian. I have a strong, ingrained Western culture in me, and I combined the elements of Indian music with my contemporary, modern, Western language.

Hindi and Urdu, both have the characteristic of using all the possible sounds that music can create, vibrating the vowels and consonants in various points of the body, from the sternum to the palate. This is an example of the richness of Indian music and culture.

A very important music festival was held in a camp next to the Kamani Auditorium in New Delhi. The table maestro Zakir Hussain was to perform in the morning concert. I was going to hear him for the first time. I will never forget the moment when I stepped on to the red carpet.

From a distance I caught a glimpse of an elegant and distinguished-looking gentleman with white hair, dressed fully in white. Even now I feel I am reliving the scene in slow motion. As I approached him, he bowed respectfully and remarked, "But you are a dancer?" He introduced himself as Harnarain Singh. He wanted to know where I was from and what I was doing in India at that time. I learnt later that he was a film producer and an influential promoter of Indian music.

It was he who introduced me to the officials of the Indian Council for Cultural Relations (ICCR), who extended an invitation to me and my company to tour India the following year. Before that the Indian government had invited Merce Cunningham and Pina Bausch to present their shows in India.

During the first trip I met Alok, a young poet in Delhi. I fell in love with him. It was he who wrote the poem *Two Tendrils of Breeze* on us. I was on my way from Delhi to Madras where I received this poem with a letter that inspired the creation of my first one-woman show, which I called *Tendrils*. I travelled across India during that long trip, immersing myself in music and dance festivals as I passed through the magnificent states of Rajasthan and Maharashtra, and the historical sites like the Ajanta and Ellora caves, and Khajuraho temples.

I spent a few days in a hotel on the beach at Mahabalipuram. One day at two in the afternoon in fierce heat, I felt a strong urge to visit the Ganesha temple near the wooded area on the beach.

Lord Ganesha, a beloved Hindu deity, known as the one who helps you to overcome obstacles was my favourite too. A subtle yet powerful energy was pushing me to go to the benevolent elephant-headed god. In the shadow of the forest, among tall and very thin casuarina trees, my body, in a moment of emotion and tears, moved in what was then the theme of movement, on which I created both *C'est ici que l'on prend le bateau* (It is here that one takes the boat), one of my most monumental and powerful shows, and *Tendrils*.

In the state of heightened emotion, I touched the cosmos with my hand, which was guiding me to create those movements.

The theme of movement from which a choreography develops, is constituted of a sequence of gestures and dynamics that arise spontaneously through improvisation. The essence of the emotions of the initial poetic idea is expressed in the theme. The strength and richness of the theme get to determine the quality of the piece.

During the creation of a theme, the artist always turns on a sort of an internal recorder that records everything that happens in the creative act. And the witness becomes energized. My experience in Mahabalipuram has left an indelible impression on me, and it has made me realize that the cosmos is always working through me.

In India, where the perception of space and time is completely different from the one in the West, one enters an altogether different dimension. I experienced in India, everything that India stood for, and I came to identify with its values. I share my primary values with Indians.

Nature is imbued with spirituality which is transmitted to the people of India. Their culture is great because it is full of humanity.

I was impressed by the way Indians listened, and how receptive and serenely analytical they were during the meetings and professional collaborations I had with them. I appreciated the way they never interrupted or crush the words of the other. There was always an atmosphere of great openness, and how they fully explored emotional nuances. They understand because the mind puts itself at the service of the heart.

Of course, this can slow down the pace, which can be a little annoying for us Westerners who are committed to the quick and effective execution of everything. The most significant intuitions, however, surface when we allow ourselves to surrender to this serene apparent slowness and recognize that a vast invisible dynamic is at work in reality.

Because of their fatalism, Indians submit to the flow of events and seem to live in a state of faith and trust rather than a state of fear. I enriched myself with spiritual, dreamlike experiences, music, musicians, knowledge, travel, temples, sculptures and paintings, and it was clear that these would influence my creativity. The artist brings her experience to her art.

My language is constantly evolving, it has never stopped, going hand in hand with my experiential and inner life.

I returned to Delhi, where Harnarain Singh gave me the keys to a rehearsal room at Kathak Kendra, the temple of dance next to the Kamani Auditorium, where I began to create *Tendrils*.

In the first piece that was born, I was sitting on the floor with my legs crossed, moving only my hands. In this dance, I tell the love story between "she" (the left hand) and "he" (the right hand). I witnessed how my hands altered before my eyes as I created.

During the creation of all the pieces of the show, I felt my body, face and eyes had changed. I experienced a physical transformation, corresponding to what was happening in the soul.

I created *Tendrils* in silence, then returned to Italy and invited two great jazz musicians Giovanni Tommaso and Luis Agudo to collaborate with the music. Luis is a well-known Argentinian percussionist who also plays the birimbao and Giovanni, a renowned bass player, is the founder of the Italian jazz-rock band Il Perigeo. I showed them the movements and the choreographies and we worked together to select the sounds.

It was a true jam session of music and dance.

It was David Zard, a man with great intuition, who introduced me to Giovanni, sensing that from the meeting an important collaboration would be born.

I believe that humans originated as androgynous beings, with male and female elements living in perfect union and complementarity before being split into opposites on earth. The realization of androgyny again is to reach the point of arrival of our soul on this planet. In my view one can meet one's twin soul, the other part of ourselves, and be the same way as we were in the original androgyny before it split, if we recognize the union of the masculine and feminine elements within ourselves again.

We have to be ready to reunite with the other original half who may have also realized the same in himself. Only when the union takes place between the two halves, that the androgyny is realized again, as in the symbol of yin and yang. It is then that the Indian symbol of unification is realized, as in the gesture of namaste.

A highly spiritual and philosophical individual has told me that only after going through this process does one become a saint, a realized entity, and returns to earth as a great master, a guru.

To those in this life who are one step closer to achieving union with the soulmate, that step is precisely in bringing together the opposites, the masculine and the feminine, harmoniously in oneself. It is a process that can only take place through spiritual purification, which includes all the dimensions of being.

Only if both souls have completed this process, their union can take place. For those like me who have this existential yearning, no other form of human love will ever be enough. Herein, it is the dance again, where I can achieve union with the One, which is the realization of my androgyny.

You know what? I believe maybe it would be better to be alone in freedom rather than suffer in relationships and be tormented by the wounds inflicted on each other. A relationship is worthwhile only between twin souls.

In my opinion, when the union of souls takes place, the cosmos explodes with joy and there is a celebration in heaven. For this to happen, however, it is necessary to awaken the spiritual energy within us. The scriptures call this energy, *kundalini* shakti, the coiled and sleeping serpent at the base of the spine.

Imagine how united souls become like a drop that has the power of the ocean in it, and that this inherent power can be released only when it sinks and becomes part of the ocean. Now try to imagine that the ocean recharges the drop of its one hundredfold power, which is the Universal Consciousness, and infuses it with its powers of omnipotence, omniscience, omnipresence, before returning it to the earth to deliver the message of love, with the mission of ferrying souls from the darkness of suffering to the light of joy.

What I told you is the fruit of my personal experience, which has permeated every cell of myself, in all the five dimensions of being. Dance has allowed me to experience the androgyny of my soul, which is why I can share this awareness with you.

Of my Indian twin soul, in whom I mirrored myself and whose name I will not give away, I would like to introduce him by first telling you that Indians perhaps because of their spiritual culture, live in joy and lightness. In contrast, Westerners are oppressed by a sense of guilt. Our culture does not prioritize spiritual values and as a result, it has lost connection with some vital values such as respect and love.

The encounter with my soulmate was a contrast of the influences that both these cultures had on both, creating in us two opposing attitudes. It was the first thing I sensed as soon as I saw him play on stage. His music was luminous and was flowing like manna, which I had seen in a dream. It has the power to awaken joy in every pore of the listener. I went to India to find all that he represented, but I suspected that he had acquired everything too easily.

The symbol of the yin-yang appeared to me; in his brightness I saw a point of darkness, just as I saw a point of light in my darkness. I immediately sensed that we were soulmates.

I anticipated that our encounter would stimulate us to face these opposite realities of our selves. I was sure he would have to go through suffering, even though he lived in a happy life situation. I, on the other hand, had to learn from him to expand my capacity for joy to overcome suffering. I feel that I have done my task and that he did it too. If our union is achieved in the next life, it will be because we have gained this insight along the way which will allow us to transcend joy, grief, dualism and antagonism to find ourselves in our union.

I remember, in fact, that as soon as I looked at him as a man rather than a musician, a critical denial of him sprang in me, undoubtedly because he was activating my atavistic fear of suffering for love: too easy, all too easy for him, spoiled, diva, pampered, Don Giovanni and Casanova, with women at his feet, a life downhill for sure. But had he reached the depths of being that I knew so well thanks to all the suffering?

I didn't even want to go and meet him, like I did with all the other musicians at the festival. However I had the strong intuition that the journeys of our lives were similar: I was from Italy and I went to find my spirituality in India, he from India and he went to prove his success in the West.

We were also associated as artists; our twin arts, music and dance, had in common the dynamic fluidity that flows like water, with the sense of play, sensuality and eroticism.

I met him again in Rome, at the RAI auditorium, after five years, and it was immediately clear to me that I was having the same reaction to him as earlier: I projected on him my usual conflict between the need for joy and the refusal to realize it. Watching him play, I felt the same critical sensation I had felt in Delhi: star, *tombeur de femmes* and self-entitled. I was proud of the agony that I had learned to manage over time; joy, on the other hand, was perilous because if it disappeared after one tasted it, one fell into an abyss.

He looked at me while playing his instrument, as if he had picked up on my critical thought, and his body drew back a little. *What antennas this genius of Indian music has!* I thought. In any case, he continued to not interest me and yet he bothered me. After the concert I went on stage to greet the manager and the other musicians to invite them to Babuccio the next day. My soulmate came up from behind and whispered into my ear, "If we have to do something, it's better to do it tonight because tomorrow I will leave."

Hmm ... Who does he think he is! I fumed silently. I ignored him without even turning around to look at him.

We women appreciate the interest of men and we are flattered by it, but it irritates us because they take our consent for granted to their initial advances, although the request intrigues us greatly. I felt only a dislike for him, yet to my amazement I was attracting him. I spent the next few days hanging out with the other musicians who remained in Rome. We had fun together for days, and they invited me to come to India to dance with them. I gladly accepted.

After a few weeks, his manager called me and said, "You know, he called me to tell me that he was very impressed with you. He learned from the others that you are coming to India to meet them and he would like to host you too..." I cut him short.

"Honestly, he's the kind of man who doesn't work for me! He is a Don Giovanni and a diva, I don't care to meet him."

The manager was stunned and he tried in every way to make me understand who he was, the importance and the greatness of the artist, but nothing made me change my mind.

Just before I left Italy, the manager was at it again, this time with an excuse. He *absolutely* had to send him a very important package, and as I was going to India, he asked me if I could deliver it to him as soon as I reached. "It would be enough if you could call him and he would come to collect it," he added. Forced in this way, I relented.

As soon as I arrived in Bombay I called the artist and, not finding him, I left a message that, given my planned departure at dawn the next day, he could pick up the package from the hotel. This way, we didn't have to meet.

I visited the other musicians in different cities until I found him in a recording studio, where he was rehearsing for a new CD. It was at that time that I was struck by his tenderness, tremendous sensitivity and magnitude of talent. This was the first time I felt a personal connection and my attitude towards him changed. I fell in love with him and then the troubles began.

I agreed to be hosted in his family home, only for a few days, since I had to leave for Ahmedabad to meet Brij Bhushan Kabra, the only musician in India who plays the guitar horizontally just like Giacinto Scelsi in Italy, while creating in *Ko Tha* (The Three Dances of Shiva).

After a few days, I returned to Bombay to see my twin soul. I danced for him in his room, from where you could see the sun going down on the Indian Ocean. I think it was the most beautiful improvisation I have ever had in silence. It is important to whom one dedicates what one creates; the dedication matters a lot and makes a significant difference.

He said he had never seen anything like it. "It is wonderful, your dance is like our music." He described all the passages of my improvisation in amazing detail and nuance; that is how good his ability to read and remember the movement was.

Indian musicians are able to memorize the dance because they visualize the music of the movements. This is why they are great improvisers and experts at being accompanists to dancers.

When his mother entered the room, I instantly felt her distrust of me, her disapproval of my freedom and permissiveness as a Western woman. I continued to improvise, reacting to her entry with humorous movements.

If we could stop time and go back and be like I am now, my life would be irrevocably bound to him forever. We would have collaborated and travelled around the world with my dance that is music seen and his music that is dance heard. We did it anyway in the soul, but not together in reality. The scriptures say that it is very rare for soulmates to meet and even more rare for them to attain union. He and I are proof of that.

He was married and I am allergic to love triangles and betrayals of any kind, given my childhood trauma. His wife was immensely valuable to him just as Guido was to me. Guido also called him a genius when he saw him play in Rome. The whole world recognized it. He was born resolved, with all his inner and outer conflicts sorted out, not only as an artist, but also as a human being.

I had a dream that while he was playing, a white liquid sprang from his hands, a kind of beneficent manna, and spread over the earth like a protective cloak. Once he told me, "You are more of an artist, while I am more social". What an honour! I believe he was right in his infinite wisdom. When I told him that the relationship between us could not work because he was married, he replied, "I am a Muslim, I can marry four times."

"Well, I am not!" I retorted.

I had another dream in which I found myself in an outdoor bar sitting alone at a table.

He was seated around 10 metres away with his wife, looking tough and masculine. They were facing each other.

All around us was silence. He got up leaving her to come to me. He took my hand, made me stand on a chair, embraced me around my hips and said, "You are my mother ... I came to get you, to take you away with me forever!" Taking my hand, he led me down to the ground, passing in front of my mother who had the expression on her face for what was happening between us. I said with compassion and love, "You see how the two of us succeeded! You should be happy."

The word "matrimony" comes from the Latin word *matrimonium*, which is a combination of *mater* (meaning mother) and *monium* (meaning action or state). It was used to describe the "condition of being a mother" and, by extension, the "state of being a wife and mother" or marriage itself. My interpretation is that the man sees his mother in his wife. Only in this way, through the love of this woman, would he be able to cut the umbilical cord with his mother. For me, it also means that man is an eternal child and woman is his eternal mother. At least in the dream, I married him.

The similarities between us also revealed our reciprocal though opposing concerns. His experience was one of being drawn back into the feminine-maternal womb of a possessive mother from whom he had attempted to flee by going from one woman to another. Mine is the one of being carried to the stars by a man, as my father did, only to let me fall into the abyss of excruciating sorrow caused by betrayal. We have both become seducers because we were afraid of the pain that comes with loving. Music and dance were the only ways we could transcend our sorrows. Following our meeting, he began to compose music.

I hope he too experienced the pangs of suffering and was able to confront it and overcome it, rather than escaping into art and success as artists often do.

I remember as a child, in conjunction with the success I had at my first dance performance, I found myself in all the newspapers of the time because I was chosen from among the students of the schools of the capital, to advertise a popular toothpaste brand, the Squibb. In that photo of mine I see him, my soulmate: as children, we were so alike! Big eyes, broad and high cheekbones, wide mouths and, above all, the same smile, which both of us have kept unchanged.

Our souls have united and in that union he has always been inside me and I know that I have always been inside him. We have amplified our energies together.

Our meeting revolutionized my life, and made me realize how much I needed to heal from my sorrow. He gave me the strength to start the wonderful inner journey through Jungian psychotherapy, meditation, yoga and EFT.

Today, I can say that I have reached the state of joy and lightness that I had aspired to, and that he represented it for me at the first glance. It is as if joy now had more value because it was, for me, the most difficult of conquests, thanks also to him.

Perhaps you would like to ask me, "Why didn't you fight for him?" Because I think it takes two to do it, I would never take a man away from another woman; I also had Guido and a sense of belonging to him. All evolution happens in its own time, and now as a woman I would like the man to strive to conquer me.

I am a free woman, and I declare with all my right that I am a symbol of freedom, not even restricted by feminism. My confrontation with him contributed greatly towards giving me the impetus to courageously embark on a complex evolutionary journey of my soul.

I deeply desire to actualize my masterpiece, which is the androgynous reunification with the other half who has my affinities in all five dimensions: spiritual, subconscious, emotional, cerebral and physical. For such a union to happen, this condition is crucial.

10

Sexuality, Eroticism and Spirituality

I believe that women get involved in a relationship to receive affection whereas men offer affection to get into a physical relationship. Though eroticism and sexuality are two different dimensions, sometimes, if carried out well, they can coexist. I am totally for eroticism. In Eros, the emotional drives are activated which permeate the entire being in all its dimensions. Truly erotic people are quite rare. They are people who are constantly in contact with their emotions, sensations, thoughts, imagination and their inner world, the soul.

I can say that the difference between sex as a mere physical act and eros is like the difference between physical exercise and dancing. Erotic is what awakens emotions at their core, in the gut, and allows you to feel viscerally. I consider sexuality to be an expression of divine energy and eroticism to be an expression of deep emotions related to spirituality, of which the body, as in dance, serves as a medium. Eroticism, spirituality and sexuality are different dimensions that should be brought together.

Life is a game, both erotic and sexual, and when the two dimensions permeate each other, it becomes spiritual. In my experience, when spirituality awakens, it merges with sexuality. By sexuality, I mean the spiritual energy that pervades everywhere and makes everything move. And here we come back to dance again. God likes it when we worship Him through the body, experiencing eroticism and sexuality through dance.

The key to happiness is reawakening one's desire to discover spiritual value. We convey our value, our joy, only when we are conscious of it. Giacinto Scelsi writes, as the fifth point in his book *Octologo*, "Between man and woman it is union, not conjoining". Union is salvific because it provides complete satisfaction whereas joining is unsatisfactory to the inner being. Feelings are something else. Most couples associate fondness with physical intimacy.

Don Jose, a well-known Andalusian theologian, once told me, "One can have fondness for a cat or chips. To wish for the best for someone is something completely different." From now on, what I will tell you, will be reflections between me and me, as if I were speaking to a friend, and I am my own best friend! I love the cosmos, the moon, the sun and the other stars. I don't need to fill a void because I am intensely connected to the source of love.

I need to share my joy to multiply it. For me, the only value is to live connected to the original source of the mystery of life and to reawaken the power of love that is hidden there, transforming surrender into a means of full realization. To dance is to let the soul to come alive and communicate through the body, just as in a real union between two individuals.

I am always ready for a union of bodies that act as instruments in a healthy dance of pleasure. To achieve this, both parties need to be there, pure and equal. Eroticism has provided me with the most intense and relevant experiences that have left an indelible impact on my life and led me to significant insights. I am polyphonic both sexually and erotically, as demonstrated by my dancing. In dancing, I always synchronize all parts of the body, be it in movement or in stillness, in each sequence. My body needs to be *played* like an orchestra! Great lovers know how to do this instinctively.

It is as if they hear the calls of various points of the body and stimulate them with intensity. They become excellent players in making the body vibrate. Sex for great lovers is an art. I can say that very few men have been able to make me polyphonically play. The man loves the woman's body, and the woman loves his love. The German word for dance is "tanzen", which signifies tension. A string can vibrate only if it is taut. I like to say it again: a man loves the woman's body, and the woman loves his love.

Courting is an art that modern man is in danger of losing. To court is to be able to enter the soul and satisfy it, putting the woman at ease, predisposing and allowing her to measure the value of man. The woman needs to be sure before opening up in the body, she needs to know how important she is to him, and it is his responsibility to reassure her at all times, by actions, gestures and words. In that way, he will recognize her value and convey it to her. No woman can resist artful wooing.

Constant attention creates the subtle connection between souls. It is for him to rise to get her. If the man fails to do this, it will mean that she is not important enough for him. Or that he has some bias towards women. Men who cannot woo are "vampires". If a man does not understand the value of what the woman is giving him and does not respect her in this exchange, he will vampirize her, drain her of her precious "lifeblood" as he is doing with Nature. Exploiting women is just like ravaging Nature.

He is destroying the world because he is not aware of the true dynamics of sexuality and eroticism, as outlined above.

The woman is humiliated in this way, so instead of supporting the man and becoming his accomplice, she will boycott him, rebelling just as Nature is doing and become sick in the body and the mind. The struggle between the masculine and the feminine is the struggle between power and love. The woman wants to let go in a man's arms, but she is afraid of losing herself rather than finding herself. The man should aspire to respect and love her instead of subjugating and possessing her. In this way, they protect each other. When we cannot express ourselves with words, we do so with the body physically, through sexuality.

For the body to be involved in this way, is natural, it is good that it is so, it is healthy to be so. In the beginning it is the body that sends messages with minimal signs and signals, and in the end the body declares that love can only be fully expressed through it. In sex the reins are in the hands of man, he is responsible for how things progress but in eroticism, the reins are in the hands of the woman, and she is responsible for it; she teaches the man how to love her.

Keeping the fire alight in a romantic relationship is exhausting and the woman is the one who often does it. In this role as a teacher of love, Eros expects her to pay continuous and subtle attention: interpreting, moving, adding, increasing, decreasing, giving the *la note* at any time. Man is a master of love in sex. Eros expects him to pay constant and subtle attention: to interpret, to move, to add, to increase, to diminish, and to always give him the "la" note.

The sexual act is an offering of oneself and not a selfish pursuit of pleasure. This is the difference between heaven and hell. The body is infinite. The hidden pleasure, in every labyrinth and particle is to be discovered with purity, respect and tenderness, even when the drums reverberate loud and powerfully during the play. What does the man give to the woman? Someone to love and educate to love her in the way she needs to feel loved in order to express herself. What does the woman give to the man? All of herself, inspiring him to express his love through his body.

Women inspire while men stimulate. Sexuality is not like drinking water; it is like sipping an elixir of long life. This is how we will reunite with God. Tantrism, an ancient Indian philosophical and spiritual movement, teaches that during sex, man has the power to stimulate and awaken the dormant pleasure in the woman's body as well as to recharge by absorbing the fluids, but not dispersing semen. In this way, the energy is pushed upwards and passes to the last chakra, where we experience union with God.

However when the energy is lived downwards, it nurtures a sense of possession and narcissism, with all that follows. The woman has the power to ignite love in a man and recharges herself by integrating him into herself. Each of us is an endless cosmos, and the diversity among people comes in the form of measurements and intensities, each with its own exclusive inner experience that is unique and irreplaceable. All humans are equal but there is no one in the world identical to another, even in a fraction of a cell. We all go through life, but in different ways and with different circumstances.

Everyone experiences the same emotions, feelings, good and evil within themselves, but with different intensities. The same happens with love. We give to others only what we have given to ourselves, and in the same way we receive from others only what we are prepared for, only after we have overcome our neediness. It is becoming increasingly clear to me that we are the ones who create the conditions for fulfilling desires. Only if we trust and rely on ourselves, does the need for protection disappear and only then can we attract those who respect us. I would not need a man from whom I need to protect myself.

On one of my long trips in India, I visited the famous temples of Khajuraho. I spent several days perceiving and contemplating their message of love. I felt like I was finally at home. The atmosphere of this sacred place seemed so familiar to me and made me feel totally at ease, as if I had always been there. It brought me out of space and time.

I read in the bas-reliefs and in the erotic sculptures of the temples, the complete opposite of the message of the Catholic culture in which I was raised, where anything about the body is considered taboo. A sick sexuality can arise from a sense of sin associated with the body.

Sexual repression produces monsters, which can take the shape of paedophile vampires even in religious circles. They live their sexuality with violence in order to express their primal inclinations, overpower through innate ownership and assert superiority. In the Tantric temples of Khajuraho, however, all possible erotic-sexual games of the body are represented with magnificent purity, in couples, in groups and even with the inclusion of animal figures, which did not bother me in the least. One cannot imagine the power of the mystical prayer that the bas-reliefs send through the merging of the bodies as a statement of love.

We are told that God wants us to be happy. Yet every time I entered a church as a child, in that gloomy and uncomfortable atmosphere, I felt that God was not as He was represented in this place of Catholic worship. I already felt that divine love is an expression of happiness, not a repression of the pleasure of the body. Eroticism, sexuality and pleasure should be experienced as a poetic homage to the Divine, which is everywhere, inside and outside of us. With this spirit, I have always lived my body, in dance, in eroticism and in sexuality.

For me, every creative act is an expression of spiritual energy. I "rock", as David Zard said, but I am also a tantric. Now I will tell you two situations that, if you are not pure enough, you could interpret as scabrous, but this is not the spirit with which I experienced them. The attitude with which we approach life's situations determines the worth and meaning of our actions.

I was in Capri with Dino Orlando, my dear Italian-New Yorker designer friend. I met him in Rome when he returned after thirty years of living in the United States. He was a man of the world always up to date on everything, highly modern and stylish, independent and tenderly unscrupulous. Throughout our long association as artists and friends, he designed the costumes for many of my shows. I adore Capri, and Dino is originally from Capri. One day, while we were sitting in the Little Square, I noticed a strange couple, a mature man with a charming James Dean beside him at a table next to ours.

We started talking. Eric, the James Dean, was Parisian, tender and brilliant, I found him erotic and fascinating. He was a young lawyer from a prestigious family. A sensual attraction was born between us, with our skins touching, in an understanding made of lightness and playfulness. Dino was happy for us, leaving us free as children to scamper around and flirt, both inside and outside the house. For the first time, I was enjoying a younger man and this could be considered a first sign of ageing.

At that time, I was thirty-five and he was twenty-four! We joyfully fed our wonderful play. Finally, he confessed that it was the first time he had felt an attraction for a woman: he was a homosexual. After a few months, he came to visit me in Rome and stayed at the Hotel Fontana near my studio, where the nights were accompanied by the roar of the water of the Trevi Fountain. He often invited me to go to France to him.

After some time, I happened to visit Veronique Bigo, a painter friend of mine, in her studio in Pont Neuf. Christo Yavachev, a well-known international artist who had created installations on many landmarks across the world, was also hosted by her when he arrived to "pack up" the Pont Neuf (bridge) with vinyl.

During that trip, one evening an Italian organizer of Indian classical music invited me to a dinner of oysters and champagne. In the middle of the dinner he told me something to provoke me, which concerned me and my Indian soulmate. It made me so angry that I left abruptly. Veronique was away from Paris. That night, I was awakened by ever stronger uterine contractions than I had ever experienced in my life until I had a spontaneous orgasm.

What would have happened if I had finished dinner without eating only half of the oysters and drinking only a portion of the champagne? I confirm that the combination of these two elements is aphrodisiac, but only if there is no additional food. After so many days spent in the Parisian Jet Set with Eric, during which time we rekindled that same magical understanding we had in Capri, it so happened that he graciously invited me to his house on my last evening in Paris.

The dinner was perfect, even better than that at the Club Concorde restaurant, regarded as one of the best in the world and quite exclusive. He had taken me there most nights and the food was so delicious that just a few bites satisfied me and each meal was a new experience. He announced that there would be a surprise that evening. After dinner, a dear friend of his, Jean Paul, joined us and he quickly became a friend of mine too. He was not homosexual; far from it, he loved women.

I think the French, especially the Parisians, are very sexy, both culturally and naturally. They have a free, compassionate and unconventional connection with sensuality, which lends lyrical value to everything. French poetry, unsurprisingly, is considered par excellence in the world.

During dinner, accompanied by the champagne that I adore, I imbibed their way of being and I let myself be tenderly carried away. We found ourselves blissfully and spontaneously making love in a threesome. Awesome! For a polyphonic woman like me, I can say that two men sexually speaking are the absolute minimum! Erotically speaking, I need a harem!

Eric with his hypersensitivity and tenderness, a radar on a woman's body, and Jean Paul with his gifted manhood, a true race horse, together we achieved the union of eroticism, made up of subtle emotional understandings with Eric, and strong bodily pleasure with Jean Paul. That night, Eric wanted to honour my femininity in this way.

The next day on the plane I felt like I was truly flying! I found myself next to Daniele Formica, a well-known cabaret actor and novelist, in whose company I felt more carefree than ever before. I was not the same person back then as I am now; when I met popular artists, I felt embarrassed because I recognized them, but they did not usually recognize me. In fact, despite being a well-established artist, I can say that I have always done everything possible to avoid popularity, as if I had always understood that in order to be renowned, one must make pacts with the devil.

My soul is not for sale. Since I learned to make deals with angels, I believe that another type of success and fame is still possible because I have gifted my soul to them. Most stars are dishonest. Very annoying. I am honest and I intend to remain so. At that time because of my experience with Eric and Jean Paul, even in dance I had a strong urge to dance against the rules of my own body language that I had developed until then. In evolution one always passes through, and goes beyond, challenging new territories of body and soul.

I want to tell you about another sexual encounter that was really different from the Capri–Rome–Paris one, even if it was somewhat unusual. I had decided to leave the usual indoor dance studio, where I worked ten hours a day between teaching courses and rehearsals with the company, and decided to hold an outdoor dance workshop amid the greenery of the beautiful Villa Borghese Park and garden in Rome. About thirty professional dancers enrolled in the course. It was a real event in the park. I had created dynamic dance sequences, replacing warm-up exercises, to gradually train the body as we moved across the park.

I had identified two ideal locations for in-depth static movement themes—at the lake and in the Campo di Siena. There were always groups of open-mouthed passers-by surrounding us. It went off very well, except that on the last day I tore a muscle.

Even years ago, at Caracas Athenaeum, Venezuela, only with the applause of the final performance did I allow myself to break my meniscus and return to Italy in a wheelchair. You see, we performers have a strong sense of responsibility and professionalism. I probably needed to stop right then and there. But I was a workaholic. Running away to work is the most common way to avoid facing oneself.

I was advised to call a massage therapist, Lillo, considered a magician among soccer players and athletes. He immediately came running to my studio in Babuccio. The pain in the groin where I had the tear was intense. Lillo was a kind, good, generous, sincere and practical man. He had a good understanding of the body, gained on the battlefield of life, and he, like me, had a natural aptitude to feel and be one with the body. He loved women and having sex was an art for him. He was an expert on the deep secrets of female sexuality.

He initiated me into techniques that confirmed to me the polyphonic nature of a woman's body. His almost scientific teachings, despite being empirical, made me fully aware of the connections among different points of the body for sexual pleasure.

The most significant discovery was that an orgasm could be reached by sucking the big toe in tandem with actions and movements in other parts of my body. Like many children, I too used to suck my big toe. As previously stated, the big toe is directly connected to the brain so dancing on the tips in classical ballet is equivalent to hammering the head. In sex, eroticism and spirituality, any manifestation of the body is well accepted, just as it is in dance, if it springs from the purity of poetry.

Sexual energy is the cosmic, divine energy that is condensed in the human body as vital energy, or the libido. In the ancient traditions of India, Shakti is the female aspect of this energy, and Shiva is the male. By sexual energy, I mean the divine energy that propels things. It is where God hides only to be found later. It is the life force that manifests itself in earthly forms.

Sexuality and eroticism are manifestations of this energy which God permits in all forms. Sin may not exist, but the inability to love oneself does because no one has taught us how. Self-love is most difficult to achieve. It is the lack of love that creates distortion and perversion. Eros is the key. The secret lies with eros. Only here on earth, we can experience this particular sensation of love. Eros brings together the high and low, the spiritual and the material, and the vertical and horizontal.

I realize my sexuality and my eroticism in each moment. When I first meet somebody, I notice their beauty and inner greatness. I see their value because I know mine, I perceive their universe because I am constantly immersed in mine. I can accept my obligation to position myself in the centre of the universe in order to absorb the cosmic energy, assimilate it and return it to myself and others as best I can at any given time. Those who do not know how to do this are ego-centric.

On this planet, the highest value is eros, or love. My capacity to love has been cultivated in proportion to my capacity to suffer. We artists are suffering experts because of our role in the world. We know well how evil lies in the unconscious, in the form of the fear of suffering, of being invaded by pain, and of not knowing how to manage it. When one learns to face these fears with courage, one is able to perceive the good and evil in oneself as well as in others, confidently encouraging the former because one is no longer afraid of being vulnerable in front of the other.

This is a conflict between fear and love. I can realize this ability in many aspects, but not in my love relationship with a man, which remains a tough knot for me. But it is because of this knot that I have such a clear understanding of these dynamics. Awareness becomes our only safeguard, strengthening the foundation of our inner core/centre.

The woman, or rather the feminine, lives primarily in art, love, ascetism and abstinence whereas the man, or rather the masculine, lives in sex, money, health and success. The meeting point of these values, which I prefer to define in the vertical (feminine) and the horizontal (masculine) is the magic of love.

One can safely say that only if there is love is it possible to realize this meeting point in the heart. What matters is that we accept others, their differences, and values as enrichment rather than expecting to find in them the same values that we already possess. It is like seeking apple juice from a lemon. In every relationship, the goal is to understand and support each other's differences to the point where we absorb them and make them our own for the sake of others; this allows for exchange and enrichment. Each gives the other what he or she is.

If you feel despised, it is because you have failed to recognize your own worth and hence stimulate the same recognition in the other. This happens in the West, but now also in the Westernized East, unfortunately. We must deal with the ego, quieten it, overcome its fears and finally surrender ourselves by trusting our hearts. The game of life in relationships is either the struggle or the harmony between power and love: power against love, the power of love, the love of power and love against power.

Harmony is achieved when these forces are fully integrated into one another, dissolving and at the same time multiplying as a result of their union. To experience the miracle of the union, both partners must go through a profound process of purification of their own desires; only then will the symbiosis of the sexual act occur, leading to true union, stillness, quietude and dynamism. Contentment lies in the valley, not in the summit.

In a journey when there is no point of arrival but only of departure, where the present moment is sufficient in itself, out of time and space, in the ecstatic pleasure, both are alone and yet together.

My mission in life is to teach others that eroticism is the highest expression of spirituality. A woman, like art, is beautiful. And like Nature, unpredictable. It is in the woman, in the feminine element, that the spiritual force lies, which can save the world and which I believe will save it.

"*Qu'est-ce que c'est de plus sage que la nudité de la femme* (What is wiser than a woman's nakedness!)!"—Max Ernst

11

My Body

During one of our conversations about spiritual mysteries, Marcello Carosi, an anthroposophic doctor, who was a mentor to me in my youth, explained to me in depth the law of karma, or the law of cause and effect. He said that this law states that the soul uses the rhythms produced by the vibrations of the emotions stored from past births to give shape to the body. It seemed to me the most beautiful of possible explanations because it was what I experienced while dancing.

My body is not only triggered by the emotional vibrations I express through movements, but I see it transforming into new curves and corresponding itself into matching forms. When I interpret the themes of my art, the body identifies with the interpretations. My body is intelligent and has an elephantine memory.

One of the most intense moments of this gift of transformation was in India when, in 1980, while I was creating a dance, expressed and realized exclusively through the hands, I saw my hands transform under my eyes and become as they are today. The fingers rise up curving backwards to open up towards the world with generosity. Have you noticed how often you see hands contracted inside, as if to clutch something?

I firmly believe that my body was created for dancing and that everything else is incidental. My body has resisted time well, maintaining its shape and sinuosity, with some minor yielding here and there —more here than there! That its skin retains its elasticity helps.

Although my body does not have the tone it had when I was dancing naked in the various ages of my youth, I would be ready to dance naked even now to demonstrate that it is still beautiful in its own way, for what it can convey even as it is.

Beauty is in the soul, in what emanates from it. I will never understand why one alters one's appearance, resorting to cosmetic surgery that distorts the original beauty that is always true.

My body is faithful, devoted and reliable. It is immune to ageing because it has understood it is the means, a channel of the energy that passes through it. In a sense, it doesn't know what fatigue is. Sometimes I look at it, naked in the mirror, and ask, "After all we've been through together, how do you handle it?"

We have a perfect union between balance and health, which we recover despite the hardships of life. Merit, in my opinion, is all about the iron discipline we have developed day after day, with small, continuous steps. My body doesn't have any form of attachment to any matter, which it enjoys every time it is given the opportunity to. It can easily fast and abstain, and it has learnt to feed on air alone.

My dear body, it was even willing to get sick for me! Disease comes when the body has no other way to stop you and warn you that you have to change your attitude towards yourself and life! You have to detach.

It took a lot of blood, sweat and tears to realize all of this. Do you have any idea how many hundreds of litres of fluids a dancer loses in her career?

Around the age of eighteen, I had an intestinal block which lasted nine months. You will say that it is impossible, that it cannot be true, but it was. I did not feel not sick, and my abdomen wasn't swollen, yet my bowel was completely blocked. I know it is hard to believe, but my body had found its own way to dispose of this "problem".

As I was no longer in communication with my parents at that time I occasionally discussed it in passing with my friends. Between the Academy and the traditional high school, I had a pretty tiring routine. I studied from morning to evening, sometimes until late at night. In the ninth month I began to worry and decided to inform my father's doctor, Iago Agostinelli, about what was happening to me.

The two Agostinelli brothers were doctors. Otello was good and humane, I felt that Mamma had been in love with him, but she would never have allowed herself an extramarital relationship. In this instance, the two brothers' names perfectly captured their personalities—or perhaps, on the contrary, their names had already defined them... *nomen omen*... who knows!

Unfortunately, Otello no longer lived in Rome, so I sought advice from Iago, who was tough and insecure. After several meetings, failing to understand the cause of this unusual phenomenon, since everything appeared regular from the examination, he suggested removing the appendix not knowing what else to do. Some allopathic doctors are so obtuse that they do not even consider that such a condition, the blockage, could be psychological and that they need to find a solution in that dimension. They just don't get it!

I wasn't afraid of any of this at the time, it is true, but I can now comprehend the mystery behind my body's reaction.

My body was able to find its harmony in disharmony and to metabolize every ingested substance, making it useful to the system without having to expel it. Today I wonder how this situation could have lasted for nine months! My body experienced an ascetic experience as if I were a yogi, but I was not aware of it then. I now realize that the emotional barriers are what "scream" their pain through the body's dysfunctions and muteness.

I was young, alone, against everyone, in an insensitive and aggressive world that could not understand me or my suffering. My loneliness and fear led to my intestinal obstruction! Someone should have helped me process all this, instead of removing my appendix which, in fact, was perfectly healthy. I underwent the surgery, and came out of the anaesthesia with great difficulty. I felt suffocated and unable to come out of the darkness. The doctor later told me that it had to be administered twice during the procedure since I was almost coming out of it during the operation. It was an absolute nightmare escaping the trauma of that anaesthesia!

It didn't end there. They tried giving me an enema because my intestinal obstruction was still there, but it didn't work because my obstructed intestines didn't release it. I saw confusion and alarm among the nurses and doctors. They then decided to use a probe from the nose down into the intestine to suck up the water and soap. The tube in my nostrils irritated my throat for hours and hours. Poor me!

My dear body! Poor thing, at nineteen it had also held up my menstrual cycle, again for a good nine months. As if it was trying to tell me in every way that I should confront my fundamental problem regarding my relationship with my femininity. May be it was not enough for me to merely dance! I felt discombobulated. But it was thanks to that block that I met Marcello Carosi, who took me under his wing and opened up new horizons, helping me understand Steinerian anthroposophy and the law of karma. He solved the problem in a matter of weeks, with a few doses of medicine and lots of love, without taking away the value of the medicine. Anthroposophic medicine takes into account the human being in its entirety. It is in the abdomen that the unconscious mind resides, the mystery, the intuition, the instinct and the will.

I had no love, a broken family, a childhood trauma of that magnitude, and I was all alone. It was as if I was pregnant with myself. I had left my first boyfriend, the second one had gone away to India, I had finished my studies and there was no great horizon opening up for an artist like me. It was inevitable—at the very least, a menstrual cycle blockage!

I would have been subjected to the most awful tortures by the different gynaecologists I saw before meeting Marcello because of their lack of understanding of the human being and the body.

Some would have forced me to get pregnant and then have an abortion, while others would have given me large doses of the contraceptive pill. All this in order to stir up my hormonal system, they tried to explain to me. They were crazy, not me. Even at nineteen, I knew that the body was a direct expression of the soul, but they were unaware of it. I slammed the door on all of them and walked away.

At the time, I was among the first to experience this unusual ailment, but I subsequently discovered that it is very common in professional, busy women. I have been the forerunner in this too. For better or for worse. Don't allopathic doctors know that the body without the soul is a corpse? So why don't they confront the disease by starting with the soul?

My dear poor feet! Considering the number of "steps" they have taken so far, it is as if they have travelled right around the world. Once I asked them to trek barefoot for ten days from Pokhara to Jhonson in Nepal. It was May, hot but not too hot and only a few of us stepped out. It was an exhilarating experience amidst nature.

In New Delhi I met the director of the Italian Cultural Institute, Franco Vincenzotti, a mountain expert, and we decided to go on this journey together. He made me buy boots that I never used. As I had been dancing for decades for eight hours a day and more, my soles were naturally callused at the time.

I persuaded Franco not to carry supplies of food as he would have liked, and we literally died of hunger. After eight hours of walking every day, a plate of rice with vegetables in the various shelters where we slept was certainly not proportionate to our caloric requirements. But we were nourished by the beauty of nature, which changed at every glance: valleys, streams, natural pools, waterfalls, cliffs, all engulfed in a sunny and mystical silence.

In spite of all that, my feet are still in harness. I am still able to dance and I am ready for anything. They have seen all sorts of things, accompanying me everywhere. They have danced almost all over the world! Healthy, though somewhat deformed by excessive work, by the toil of living and by time, they are, in their own way, beautiful. They too, like me, find their harmony in disharmony. Beauty is not in the form but in what emanates from it. In that inner beauty lies the mysterious secret of life. My feet emanate their own lives with grit and eroticism.

The foot is the most erogenous point of the body, and in some cultures it is considered the most sacred. In India, it is customary to worship the guru's feet because this is where the mystery of spiritual energy resides. According to reflexology, the entire organic system is gathered in this area of the body. In astrology too, the sign of Pisces, considered to be the most spiritual, resides in the foot. The knees are the release point between the will (the unconscious), the mind (the intention) and the desire. Whenever our will goes against desire by making choices which go against it, the knees are affected. I am a tangible proof of this.

While I was touring across India with the great maestros of Indian music, I ruptured my meniscus. It was a serious injury and every city we landed in we consulted the best orthopaedician who somehow manipulated the tibia and fibula to get the knee back into action.

Having fallen in love with what I considered my twin soul, but to whom I did not want to surrender myself as he was married, my body made me "snap" the meniscus, to force me to understand that it no longer wanted to just dance but also to love. It wanted me to live as a woman and not just as an artist. My inner existential battle, in which the will rejected the desire, was triggered during that journey.

Many years later the same happened in the United States. The orthopaedician Giancarlo Puddu, nicknamed Ginocchiaro (*ginocchio* meaning knee, so "he of the knee", operated on me when I returned to Italy in a wheelchair. I was in a similar dilemma. At that time, I was infatuated with a well-known American hatha yoga teacher, who too was a much-married man. As an instructor of anusara yoga, he was legendary. Our relationship was very subtle, discreet (it was not clandestine, but subtle as in *sukshma* … on a different plane) and exclusive.

Falling in love awakens the desire for what we "desire", the absolute that we lack because it lies dormant within us. I am always in love with something or someone and I am grateful to the cosmos for this gift—to be so even when I suffer. Somehow I have a deep fondness for suffering. I dive into it, as if I were crossing water and letting it flow through me. I play with it like I play with life. The state of death is the state of pure vibration of the soul free from the chains of the body.

Because we feel such strong emotions when dancing and falling in love, we are able to transcend our bodies and achieve detachment. I know how to share everything; when I share joy, it multiplies, when I share sorrow, it dissolves. I love those around me but I am disappointed when I find that they don't do the same for me, they don't know how to love. We desire things that we haven't yet been able to obtain, and once we do, the desired thing becomes a part of ourselves. Insecurity, due to a lack of confidence, creates the fear of not being able to realize our desires and that is what makes it impossible to actually realize them. Only when this fear is conquered does everything happen on its own, seemingly by a miracle. It is the strength and intensity of aspiration that guide us towards their realization.

The scriptures teach us that deep feelings give meaning to life. The fear of not being able to succeed and the fear of suffering, pushed me to overcome the fear. I wish with all my heart that you will be able to be in touch with your capacity to feel what is happening inside yourself.

When the heart is there, it always bleeds, but it is only by bleeding that it regenerates itself continuously. Otherwise it will dry up.

Also in the relationship with food, the attitude with which we approach food is important.

I have never seen my mother cook; she delegated it to the domestic helpers, but the rare times she prepared food it was strange, inedible Milanese slops that smelled horrible, like a boarding school canteen. I am sure that if I hadn't inherited this model from her, I would have been an excellent cook. But I still don't choose to cultivate this "natural talent" which I am supposed to have according to all my astrological readings.

From the age of fourteen, when my mother left home, I ate in bars or takeaways on the move and even today I would have done the same but I am more disciplined now so I don't do it anymore. Since I was a teenager, I developed a difficult and conflicted relationship with food. I had already made dance my life and I could not afford to fatten up or weigh myself down by eating.

We athletes work hard with the body, just as with everything else. Stress in "normal" people plays the same role, generates the same fatigue. After eight hours of training and rehearsals, there is not much energy left to digest and metabolize—processes that are easier to carry out at rest.

This is one of the main reasons why athletes need to follow strict dietary guidelines. And so it was for me too. In short, I was always on a diet, and looked at food as an enemy. That is no longer the case; for many years now I have had a good relationship with food, especially when it is cooked by others. I listen to my body, giving it only what it needs, a lot or a little, everything or nothing, according to the moment and the mood.

The body is an expression of the soul not only in its relationship with food. In fact, it is the soul which dictates all our choices in everything we do.

"Whatever you can do or dream you can, begin it. Boldness has genius, power and magic in it!"—Goethe

What I am about to tell you now is dedicated to all those who are struggling to lose weight: never tell your body that you will put it on a diet because it will feel threatened, it will raise its guard, it will feel punished and deprived, and as a reaction, will hysterically absorb everything that you give it, even the air.

Tell it instead that you intend to take care of it by giving it what it really needs and persuade it delicately, with kindness and love. "From today, I'll give you everything you need to eat, all the food you want and that will make you feel good." With this reassuring message, the body will be satisfied even with only fruits and vegetables.

In modern culture, the art of listening to the body has been lost; we are no longer educated to hear what happens to it. In fact, we have also not been educated to feel emotions. These poor bodies are often left to gain weight without any movement, with the mind that is projected onto the external world, working to achieve something at any cost, affirming one's ambition and thus filling the void, and compensating for this weakness by filling up with food.

In fact, the body needs little food and a lot of movement. It is the temple where to find God, but only if the body is healthy can He be found. Otherwise, you will be able to find Him only at the point of death because finally the soul will be detached from a sick body, tired of living.

Daniele Masala, a Pentathalon gold medallist at Los Angeles, and I met during my 1988 Olympic participation in Seoul, where I was asked to dance at the Olympic Arts Festival held concurrently with the games. In our conversations on almost everything, I was astounded to discover that we shared a common route in the soul-body relationship as well as in our relationship with food—carbohydrates for lunch, proteins for dinner, etc.

Both of us needed the same things—to stretch and strengthen our muscles during our training and striking the perfect balance between the two. Once again, the male and the female dimensions have to come together in a balance.

I reaffirm that one can gain weight by fasting and lose weight by eating, according to one's inner state of being. Although a dancer, I was an Olympian. Life is an athletic challenge for everyone, but only for a few it becomes an Olympian challenge.

When I create or fall in love, I no longer need food and while living on air alone, I feel full of energy. But when I have moments of inner emptiness, I gain weight even if I am fasting. This happens because the happiness-generating endorphins are absent.

I had never felt the urge for sweets until I spent a considerable amount of time in an ashram in India. I declare that I have never loved sweets. Luckily for me, not only do I not like sweets, I find them actually nauseating. On that occasion however, it really hit me hard. I ate whole pies, gobbled any kind of pastries, feeling sick if I didn't start again after a few hours. The ashramites had given me the nickname Bandharananda, since *bandhara* in Sanskrit means banquet and *ananda* means bliss.

I could do nothing. My body's reaction to what was happening to me on the inside could not be stopped. Disillusionment and betrayal in love, both in this life and previous ones, had filled me with emptiness and thrown me into the abyss.

I returned to Italy with ten extra kilos and a backside that Guido described as being as big as a TV. Fortunately, everything happens for the best.

In the years that followed, I not only confronted that void and found a solution during my amazing introspection, but I also met a dietician who pointed out to me that salt and milk were my food foes at the time. Like my father, I would have run the risk of having a heart attack, from too much salt. Let's say that the insatiable craving for sweets compelled me to confront the reason why it was released in my body and soul.

Dear friend, my dear friend, if you can't lose weight, it is because you need to fill a void, which instead of food, should be filled with your love for yourself. This is prevented by feelings of guilt, worthlessness, anger and above all by the fear that you have allowed to grow in yourself, because you did not receive love when you felt you deserved it from others.

Love needs to be continuously renewed as adults from the inside out, and not the other way round. The solution is not "to gobble up" whatever pleasure life has to offer us on the outside, as this will make the chasm harder to cross. Rather, by unearthing the original source of life that is love. We not only realize it in ourselves, but we let it "overflow" onto others.

One of the most exhilarating experiences in the way of feeding myself was with macrobiotics. Guido and I decided to try this adventure. Via Monte della Farina was the only macrobiotic restaurant in Rome in the 1970s. In name and in practice, Providence was a Sicilian cook who used her culture and culinary expertise to create remarkable, albeit strictly macrobiotic, dishes. We went there daily for our lunch and dinner for about a year, except when we were on tour, of course.

We had never been this good. With Guido food and everything to do with it was always a fun experience. This time we laughed about our new adventure together. We perceived it as the laughter derived from the purification of the system and the renewed sense of well-being. In that period I created *Apotropia*, based on the music of Frank Zappa, which was the most exhausting choreography I had ever done. It is safe to say that the only way to dance it without dying is to be on macrobiotics.

Marcello Carosi had been dead for many years. So a friend of mine referred me to Antonio Negro, the luminary of homeopathy in Italy, who treated me until the end. He was 101 years old when he left this planet. Antonio Negro was an incredible soul. He entered you like a laser and observed every detail of your life.

At the first meeting, I cried, moved by what he said about me. He immediately understood the reason for my hypothyroidism the reason why I had gone to consult him in the first place.

Antonio Negro was an endocrinologist before he took to practising homeopathy. He told me that in my case this dysfunction was due to a great pain, a childhood trauma that I had responded to with great rancour, unknowingly. The liver is the organ where anger resides, and the functioning of my liver had been severely disrupted, putting a strain on the thyroid, which controls metabolism. As you are already aware, the trauma he was referring to was related to my connection with my father.

He spoke as if he had known me forever, though he had never met me before and no one had given him any prior information. He said that I was an exceptional artist and that I had an inner sensitivity and an infinite universe within me, but that only through love and union with a man who could fully understand me, would I fully realize my self. He concluded by saying, "I wish you to find a man who really understands you."

He took me off the very high doses of Eutirox I was taking, stating that the thyroid needs to be respected, it does not need a foreign ingredient to replace it. According to him if the whole system had been working well, even if the function of the thyroid was reduced it would not have caused any imbalance in me. And so it was.

He treated my liver with *Natrum Muriaticum*, but one must be cautious here. For in homeopathy, a particular substance can affect different persons in different ways, depending upon each one's psychosomatic characteristics.

The year-long process of eliminating the Eutirox was a long and difficult one. I sometimes called Professor Negro and begged him to put me back on Eutirox because I was feeling very ill, but he charmingly persuaded me to hold on, to resist because I would recover even without the Eutirox. I was a heroine! I managed to resist, thanks to his conviction, help and support.

Marcello Carosi had once told me, "The real heroes are those who resist."

I would not like to bore you with stories of too many diseases, but these last ones could be useful to better understand the role of disease in the relationship between the body and the soul.

The next two new illnesses took place in India due to my recklessness. I drank litres of water in Trivandrum, Kerala. It was an unintentional attempt at suicide! They say that the water of this city is the most polluted in the country. It gave me a serious liver infection.

I had fallen in love with a dancer of the company. I had resisted heroically and I had not given in. I always say that it is forbidden to weave love stories with collaborators, as it is neither professional nor manageable, but on that occasion I used professional ethics to "hide behind a finger".

I was afraid of experiencing a strong passion, the strongest I had had until then.

Trivandrum was the last stop on the tour of seventeen cities in India. I planned to stay back by myself and heal the wounds of my love-sufferings after the rest of the company returned to Italy.

An excellent doctor in Delhi treated me with homeopathic medicines, but I remained unwell for more than a year.

Years later, in a difficult period, you know the ups and downs of artists, I contracted an amoebic infection on a trip to the famous caves of Ajanta and Ellora. Marcello Carosi had treated me by giving me injections of gold in the abdomen, which when combined with an anti-amoeba diet created a situation of total purity in the intestine, which he said would become like that of a newborn. He explained how in this way the amoeba, which recreates itself when it opens and splits, not being able to feed, would have become extinct by itself. Very subtle war strategy! Due to this type of covert presence in the bowel, I too won this war after a very long period of exhaustion for my entire body.

The body is the soul. It should be treated with respect, love and thoughtfulness, never with violence, even when dealing with illnesses. However, allopathic medicine attacks it as evil, waging war on it, thereby weakening the whole organism.

The truly salvific approach is the exact opposite: to support, strengthen, purify the immune system, understanding and elaborating the cause of the disease, so that the concentration of evil dissolves by itself, finding no more bread for its teeth. When viewed in this light, the illness becomes a chance for development and fortification. It even serves a constructive and restorative purpose since it allows one to better and cleanse oneself, as well as learn to embrace and love who they are.

This is the attitude with which one should face any difficulty in life.

Can you see how all my ailments are attributable to that blockage in my childhood and how they have really arisen from that?

It is that deep sorrow that attracts the conditions to perpetuate the same sorrow but I hadn't been able to break that chain then, as I have finally done now.

Everything has changed today because I can respond to the situations differently because I no longer hold any self-limiting ideas and I am not constrained by the negative effects of fear and wrath.

What age am I now?

I feel I have no age because I live all ages: six for the will to play, sixteen for the attitude towards future projects, twenty for matrimonial ones, twenty-eight for spiritual ones, forty in physical energy, eighty in wisdom, a hundred as a lived experience, and sexually forty-two, the age of suicide or rebirth, according to Steiner.

Regarding the physiological age, Yogananda, a great teacher, maintains that we must not identify with that and I love to follow the teachings of the great.

All life is before me, even if it should only last another day or month. This is the attitude with which I live every moment. Isn't the momentum you build up before you fly, a weakness? This is true both in dance and in life!

I'll be turning "— ty" soon.

12

Self-Healing Tools

Both dance and therapy are ways of descending into the root of life and consequently into the root of joy and sorrow. Dance sublimates pain transforming it into joy, while therapy dissolves and resolves it. Suffering pushes the artist to create while dance makes the artist feel joyous and liberated. The journey in both is to reach the roots, but the motivations to go there are different. From a young age I felt as if I was absorbing the grief of the world around me, as do many artists. Today, I am aware that this trait in me is also a shamanic quality with which I was born.

Aura is the energy that emanates from the soul and envelops each one of us. Every aura has its own characteristics which are expressed in colours. In this regard, I will tell you of an incident that took place in a friend's villa during a private meeting with a Swiss doctor who used the Kirlian camera, which can photograph auras.

We must have been about twenty people there. The doctor photographed the aura of each one of us and followed it up with a private session to explain it. With me, she began by saying that she had never seen an aura with such therapeutic powers, which I was unaware of at the time. It was emerald green in colour, expanding into white, with an orange area down to the right corner. She explained that the emerald green indicates the healing power of those who absorb negative energy and transform it into positive energy; the orange zone, on the other hand, indicates my aggressiveness, which was actually a salvation in my case, she added, and explained how throughout my life, aggression has served as an alarm and a drain valve, without which I would have been suffocated by all the negativity absorbed within me.

Through the spiritual practices that I have assimilated over the years, I manage to release the pain I absorbed and put my talent at the service of others, rather than be crushed by it. Although I choose to present myself alone in the world, I never feel alone because of the magical encounters with special people whom I attracted to myself and to whom I was attracted.

As I have mentioned earlier, I was nineteen years old when I first learned about anthroposophy, the science of the spirit founded by Rudolph Steiner. Anthroposophy and homeopathy have similar principles. Steiner is considered a clairvoyant and a spiritualist, who gave illuminating insights on medicine, pedagogy, painting, sculpture, architecture, music and dance.

In dance he created Eurythmia which I studied at the Goetheanum, an anthroposophical facility in Dornach, Switzerland. Eurythmia is an artistic expression that Steiner recommended as treatment for certain diseases. Eurythmy is a series of continuous dynamic movements that I have assimilated in my dance style. It marked a significant shift in my language as an artist. The uninterrupted movement was no longer sculptural and plastic, but dynamic. It is a natural language of the body, as highly spiritual as all of Steiner's work.

Anthroposophic medicine has always had a significant impact on me. As I previously mentioned, I used it to cure amoebiasis that I contracted in India. Steiner is very close to the East, to India and to Theosophy.

Anthroposophy links the East to the West. My knowledge of Indian culture began with reading his books.

When I arrived at the large atrium in the Goetheanum, I found many people gathered there. A tall lady with white hair and an aristocratic appearance came up to me and said, "We need artists like you who can revitalize the language of Eurythmy. Here there are academics who slavishly try to codify Steiner's indications without revitalizing them."

She didn't know who I was, I hadn't introduced myself yet, but I felt that this woman, like Steiner, was a clairvoyant. She was the director of the Eurythmia department and a former Italian dancer of La Scala in Milan.

Despite the privilege and honour of this invitation, I did not feel like adhering totally to that language, unlike yoga with which I feel a sense of complete belonging. The same happened with the shamans of the Siberian tantric yoga, whom I met in Germany and who recognized me as one with the same powers as them. They asked me to follow them in their mission in the world. Even on that occasion I didn't feel like joining them.

With Carosi, I learnt the law of karma. Analyzing the symbols, the signs and meanings of what happens in our lives allows us to link the present to everything in the past from which the present has actually sprung forth. In every malaise and suffering, physical or mental, there is an emotional, existential, karmic purpose that manifests itself. So I began my mission to find India, which was already inside me. That was when I became aware of the philosophical and spiritual value that the culture of that land could bring to my life.

The rich tradition of India is based on the understanding of mind and body. From what I understand, some of the ancient Indian wisdom engages with matters related to what we call psychoanalysis today. For more than five thousand years, India has revealed the secrets of the mind and of the unconscious.

Yoga meditation is another universe; it leads directly into the dimension of the self, the higher plane, whereas psychoanalysis brings one into the mystery of the unconscious where the self is yet to be discovered. In addition to yoga meditation, I studied hatha yoga in India and New York. I have been practising it for over thirty years and I am also an instructor in it. This discipline has enabled me to heal the damage that dance techniques and sports had caused to my body.

While practising hatha yoga, the *prana* reaches every cell of the body through the breath, and the body–mind consciously realizes the union in which the energy flows, healing all that there is to heal. The wisdom in this thousand-year-old practice was transmitted directly through inspiration from cosmic energy, with which man was still in direct contact.

I began hatha yoga with my friend Rossana Rizzi Silva, who taught at her extravagant Appia Antica villa, one of the oldest and most beautiful streets where you can still breathe the Roman life as it was. The house was charming because it had a restored train car and a swimming pool on a large lawn, which added to its charm.

Rossana invited me to try her classes. I never say no to anything that attracts my innate curiosity and spirit of adventure. Although the course was attended mostly by ladies and therefore extremely elementary, I discovered a new way of accessing the body, with a passive rather than active attitude, as in dance.

In India, I studied Iyengar Yoga, which, like dance, involves experiencing movement mentally, with precise analytical indications for each area of the body, always consciously combined with the breath. Many years later, when I devoted myself to the asthanga yoga led by Pattabi Jois, I discovered that he and Iyengar had trained in the same ancient method of yoga. Iyengar later broke away to create his own style which, in my opinion, having developed a more rational attitude, has lost the natural and spontaneous origin of postures that asthanga yoga has maintained.

My conclusion on hatha yoga is that the asanas are the same in all styles; what changes is the order in which they are practised, the duration for which the poses are held and the attitude with which they are felt, which determines how to experience them within. The images that one visualizes and sends to the body are the very thoughts that power the asanas. This determines diverse styles and their effects on individuals who perform them.

I spent decades in New York State studying anusara yoga, which is one of my favourite styles. I also attended an anusara yoga retreat for teachers in London, but the teacher, a very tall man with a rigid body seemed to be prejudiced against me throughout the course. It was as if he was resentful of my elasticity. It was also evident to me that he found it annoying because I was an established artist in dance, an art form that uses the human body exceptionally.

He was projecting all his frustrations on to me, and he entered into a competition with me although I had a pure and humble attitude. He did not want to give the teacher certificate despite the fact that I was the most experienced hatha yoga practitioner at that retreat. Not that it mattered to me. I had attended the retreat for personal enrichment, not for the certificate. For me, every yoga class is an opportunity for improvement.

Each master communicates with his unique insight and nuance; the body is boundless, and one never stops learning it. Even though I am a hatha yoga instructor, I continue to learn with wonderful teachers whenever and wherever I have the opportunity.

I built my life and profession on my natural talents, keeping them alive, never taking them for granted and working on them every day. An artist does not need academic recognition. Think about it, I never even picked up the degree from the Dance Academy since I didn't know what to do with it!

During my long journey in yoga, I also went through Jungian psychotherapy. This other journey, which lasted ten years, three sessions a week, began with the interpretation of dreams, symbols and oneiric signs before progressing to the treatment of psychological discomfort and pain. My psychoanalyst was Lanfranco Marra, a Neapolitan, a sharp man who could map the meanderings of the soul. Before becoming a psychoanalyst he was a lawyer. He explained to me at the first meeting that one cannot enter the circles of hell, the unconscious, without a guide. Dante also needed Virgil!

Psychoanalysis is a cognitive experience of self, it dissects and analyzes the problem. Thanks to my good karma, I also had the humility to confront and understand my severe neurosis. In my experience, psychoanalysis provides the opportunity and the ability to know how to manage problems, but it does not always solve them. I enriched myself with its value which was to give me awareness of the root of the problems. To solve them, in my opinion, spiritual tools that go beyond the rational dimension are needed.

My involvement with psychoanalysis has been tiring, but I can say that it has also been one of the most beautiful and mysterious journeys even though it took me excessively into the mental dimension, which is not ideal for a woman like me who is already very much there. Anyway, if I were to go back, I would do it again.

Rationality is activated in an exaggerated way when it investigates unresolved problems in the unconscious dimension, where the original source of pain resides. As in my artistic process, as in spiritual practices, I have always gone beyond the mind.

This extremely complex process sometimes led me to experience such intense pain and into such difficulty to overcome it that I could no longer create. Between the ages of thirty-three and forty-three, I often suspended my activity to face my inner demons. They were years in which I appeared and disappeared from dance. I plunged myself in Dantesque abysses through psychoanalysis, and by living in the ashrams in India. I was shuttling between India and Rome. I believe that an artist is a pain expert like all those who have a hyper-sensitive, hyper-receptive and hyper-fragile soul.

I needed psychoanalysis at the time, but I now recognize its limitations. The artist creates symbols and signs. Psychoanalysis certainly helped me to refine my ability to interpret them as well as recognize them in daily life. Jung had come to understand the collective unconscious in which, he said, God himself existed. We are the microcosm in the macrocosm.

We give others only what we first give to ourselves. We project what we are on the external world. We have a great responsibility, first of all towards ourselves. What we gain for ourselves becomes our contribution to the others, which then reaches out to the cosmos, only to return to the world again.

If you want to give love to others, you must first take on the full responsibility of loving yourself. It might seem a contradiction, but this is the altruism that replaces narcissism. One appears to do so, but without even realizing it, one stops at the superficial appearance of things, never really seriously playing the game of life. One falls into the presumption of believing that one is giving love while in reality one is asking for it, even demanding it. Most often one masks this unrestrained yearning for love by offering too much, causing it to be a burden on the other.

Narcissus was complacent in his beauty. The same is true for the fake artist: narcissism displays an inability to get into the secret essence of things, grasp its core, and convey it as an absolute value, eliciting the same emotion in the observer. When this happens in human relationships, they too are false and are doomed. We shut ourselves up in our own little self, blaming external circumstances and others for what happens to us.

The ideal would be to understand pain by activating the ability to love ourselves, accept ourselves as we are and forgive ourselves for our human limitations, and then do the same with others. We give others our truth, our inner reality. When we believe we are giving love but instead we demonstrate the falsity of our narcissism, the ego manifests itself, not the self.

C. G. Jung, the enlightened psychoanalyst, had predicted that in the coming decades humanity would have spiritual therapeutic tools to achieve results, which was unimaginable at that time.

The most effective therapeutic tool, among all those that I have encountered and experienced in my travels around the world, has been the Emotional Freedom Techniques, also known as tapping or EFT.

I sought psychoanalysis because I felt the need for a tool that would allow me to enhance my ability to interpret dreams, as I had been having an abundance of fantastic dreams every night for years. As for my engagement with EFT, I did not seek it out on my own. Radisha introduced me to this therapeutic practice. The first time I experienced EFT a physical pain I had at that time immediately disappeared. Fascinated and intrigued, I studied this technique for years, with the same passion with which I immersed myself in everything. I went to New York to work with Carol Look, one of the most prominent EFT practitioners in the country. I received my EFT practitioner certification in 2008.

In my opinion, psychoanalysis and EFT are complementary tools. I have used them by integrating them into the path I had taken in Steiner anthroposophy. I would say that each of these tools has a specific and fundamental role. Jungian psychoanalysis, also known as analytical psychology, incorporates the reading of symbols and signs into EFT. The symbols are nothing more than the mysterious expressions of emotions. In fact, EFT is also practised by psychoanalysts, psychologists and psychiatrists mostly in the United States.

EFT removes unconscious emotional blocks and elevates one into the lightness of spiritual energy, or the self. When emotional blockages are eliminated, self-care takes place. The body heals itself through the soul, just as the suffering soul had made the body sick. Here it is the game of balance between the psyche and the body.

At the core, we are perfect. This perfection is gradually suffocated, buried and caged by the limiting beliefs created by the lack of love we have experienced. We come to this earth to experience love; when we do not receive it, we react with fear, anger, guilt and contempt. Removing, means eliminating the restricting effects of these reactions and restoring our original perfection, which is love for ourselves and for others, of which we are naturally capable. Free will is what makes us the authors of our lives.

The mind transfers thoughts into the body, resulting in well-being or "ill-being" according to their emotional and vibrational qualities. When the mind is completely conditioned by the unconscious dimensions that have yet to be processed, it can manifest as illness.

It is the mind that creates illness and it is the mind that treats illness through purification, or self-redemption. This allows you to keep a high energy level in which everything is possible.

This technique can help you overcome any emotional, physical or psychological impediment. For me, EFT is the most subtle and powerful therapeutic tool we have in the world today.

EFT involves talking about the problem while self-stimulating the Chinese acupuncture meridians and tapping with fingertips on precise places on the hands, face and chest. By stimulating these points, we move from the mental dimension to the emotional dimension, thus opening up the energy flow channels into the unconscious. It is clear that the answers do not come from the mind but from the emotion itself. It is precisely because the word does not spring from the mental dimension but from the emotional one, that EFT has the function of a laser that burns pronounced emotionality.

With this stimulation, identifying and stating the emotion that had provided the blockage is the key to freeing it. According to Indian yoga, chakras are energy centres that house many emotions. The energy branches off throughout the body through the *nadis*, which correspond to the Chinese acupuncture meridians used in EFT.

For example if you are suffering from betrayal or abandonment, using EFT to address this pain can lead you further and deeper until you learn that the reason of the betrayal or abandonment is also within ourselves, not only in the other. We begin to work on the emotions that emerge: anger, fear, loneliness and we are able to uncover childhood anxieties and distrusts that arose as a result of a lack of recognition of our value expressed via love when we still needed to receive it from others.

Anger stems not from being betrayed, but from not feeling loved. With EFT, anger dissolves because it is replaced, on a deep emotional level, with acceptance, love and forgiveness for ourselves. I want to emphasize that in this way, as adults, we become parents to ourselves, capable of understanding who we are and what we deserve.

Even psychoanalysis works in this way, guiding us down the same path, but fails to dispose of all the emotions that gradually emerge, as EFT does. Any experience in adult life that causes a block can be resolved with EFT, not in the rational dimension, but in the unconscious one, which resides in the belly. The obstacles that are saved within, melt softly and dissolve lightly with EFT.

The EFT process is delicate, respectful and easy. The good practitioner knows how to ask the right question, at the right time, resulting in the articulation of the proper word that has a cathartic effect. The emotional dimension is subtle, thus it must be identified and expressed using the appropriate words, the right nuances.

Indian culture teaches us how the word has immense power. The repetition of the mantra gives strength to the content that is repeated, making it vibrate inside and strengthens it. The repetition of the mantra, which is the repetition of the divine name, ensures well-being. Psychoanalysis uses the word to understand the problem. But while repeating the story of pain feeds the introspective investigation and expands its awareness, it also reinforces it and amplifies it.

Because of the ten years of Jungian psychoanalysis, when I lead the EFT sessions, I rely on the ability I have acquired to enter the mysterious dimension of the human soul, in a subtle/light and intangible way. In this process, the mind observes without being rationally activated. It becomes the detached witness.

In each session with the people who rely on me, I relive the joy of seeing their anguish dissipate. I can state that it is the same satisfaction and joy that I feel when I dance because dancing is abandoning oneself to emotions and freeing them.

Here is the added pleasure of seeing my strong belief realized: that the fundamental step for resolution in every aspect of life is to trust and entrust. In dance and EFT, the pain melts in the fire of love. I feel that these two professions complement and enrich each other by weaving together the creative and the human elements.

The seeds of our past lives are found in this life, from the moment of birth and throughout existence. Everything about the environment of childhood, including our parents, sisters and brothers, relatives and places, and the world in which we live, reflects the essence of our past life. It is only after the sixth year of life that the conscious self begins to develop. Everything up until that point has occurred entirely in the unconscious dimension It is in this dimension that the karmic seeds of previous lives are rooted. We need to return to our childhood beliefs in order to solve them and reliably retrace them.

In solving the issues of the current life, those of the previous lives are also resolved. This is why I think that to cleanse the roots of the unconscious, it is not necessary to undergo past life regression therapy. This confirms that our spiritual essence is played on the vertical, and our realization in reality, on the horizontal. For me, the cleansing of the roots is the most important aspect for the well-being of our existence and realization.

This purified state allows for the union of the masculine and the feminine, internally as androgyny and externally as the union of a couple. If you do not have a purified root, your tree will collapse.

The Creator empowers us to shape our lives by the choices we make in each moment, allowing us to do whatever we want by establishing our own chain of cause and effect. It is the law of free will. It is we who have created the conditions for sorrow as well as for joy, success and satisfaction in our lives. In this life we face the consequences of our actions, which is why we are responsible for what happens to us while also creating the conditions for future events. This is our karma.

Following one of my EFT sessions with a young man, dramatic and atrocious events emerged, of which he was a victim of as a child. I began to meditate to dispose of and purify myself of all his pain that I had absorbed. I was so disturbed that as soon as I closed my eyes and took deep breaths, an overwhelming rage towards the Creator erupted in me,

How can you allow so much pain? Why did you create a world where one suffers such atrocities? Why did you create this game of life to include such pain? At that moment, I realized that we create the circumstances of our lives, for better or worse.

I need to make peace with the self and overcome the fear I have of surrendering completely, and letting go in love, to understand why evil is allowed to exist. Every animate and inanimate thing exists due to the Divine will. What motivated God to include the element of evil and suffering in the game of existence? He could have created a game where there was no need for so much sorrow or wickedness. He allowed the evil in the human being to exist through acquiring knowledge with the mind instead of the heart, understanding rather than experiencing and comprehending. It is the ego that creates fear in the mind of losing itself in the love of God that resides in the heart.

Is knowledge too, obtained by eating the apple from the tree, created out of the power of His love? Certainly, knowledge gained through the mind is antagonistic to love and yet is not something different from Him. He allows the fear of surrendering to exist. The idea that God has created a game in which anyone can create pain makes me distrust and fear Him.

I need an act of faith. What is faith? It is trust in which fear that comes from the ego dissipates in the heart. Sometimes, we can lose faith in God because of so much of misery in the world. That is how it has been for me. As a child, I unconsciously developed a dread of suffering rather than the capacity to trust and love.

I descended into the root of the fear that my ego has of abandoning itself to the love of God; it was the same fear that I had experienced at the age of seven. I did not trust Him because He allowed me to suffer. This, I believe, is the fundamental problem with respect to God that every human being must resolve in himself, not in the head but in his inner being where the will resides.

I have always understood the meaning of suffering and its contribution to our growth. Where does this element of evil and suffering, which God allowed to exist and allowed to continue to be part of the game of living, come from? Why was the Tree of Knowledge there in Paradise, tempting one to eat its fruit? And then there is the mind that creates suffering in the heart where joy resides.

In this life, we are born to deal with the challenges that we have not yet overcome in our previous lives. The child knows what suffering is because he experiences it in its entirety, without any protection and points of reference, because he does not have a fully formed consciousness. As a child, I was aware of all this intuitively. I believe that in childhood we know everything through intuition and the unconscious, but are unaware of it. It is like we have another brain in the belly. I understood that I should go there to resolve my suffering.

In my experience, hypnosis does not cleanse the unconscious. I underwent three hypnotic sessions with Chris Gricomson, in Santa Fe, New Mexico. It was revealed that in my previous birth, I had been a *castellano*, the wife of a rich, powerful and good man who loved me deeply. I was quite generous and engaged in good work, especially for children. Envious enemies had killed me with poisoned needles hidden in my clothes. Whether it is true or not, they are certainly symbols that correspond to my current reality. I have never been able to deal with envious people and instead of protecting myself from them, I rebel and provoke them, making things worse.

We must protect ourselves from ourselves, since the external world is a projection of the inner world. They who love us should help protect us from our inner foes. To know and to understand is fundamental, but that is not enough to burn the karmic seeds that are the essence of our previous lives. Unprocessed issues cause us to generate conditions that match to them in real life. The therapeutic solution is to heal the blocks in the unconscious dimension created by instinctive reactions to emotional dynamics.

The unconscious is St Patrick's well where the seeds of former incarnations are gathered, together with their own karmic history. It is the ego that creates personal hell. In my experience, every time I remove the source of pain, I let the seeds of love breathe inside me. I do not believe that a full spiritual realization is possible without a total purification of the unconscious.

If a mother has not purified it within herself, she will undoubtedly transmit her inner vibrations onto her child. The youngster unwittingly absorbs all the vibrations that emanate from the parents and others around him, as he has no defence or protection yet. The work we have to do on ourselves is to get rid of the negative vibrations we have absorbed from the outside world: anguish, anxiety, guilt, neurosis and suffering.

Western culture does not teach us how to enter the unconscious mind. What is needed is a religion that can help us comprehend and heal our emotional turmoil. Instead, religion is merely teaching us rules and dogmas that often do nothing but cultivate repression, prejudices and taboos about the body, sexual energy and inner freedom.

Repressions in the collective unconscious reveal themselves through ongoing violence, and underground fires smouldering beneath the ashes burn in an obscure manner, resulting in irreversible ruin. If the anguish is left to hatch inside and is not processed, it becomes repressed and eventually manifests as physical or mental illness.

Healing leads to lightness and joy. It is a matter of bringing to the surface the true nature of a human, which is joy, freeing it from the heaviness of internalized pain. This is what our purpose of life is.

Sometimes after having got rid of the anger, for this game that includes pain, I know even if I don't completely understand it, that pain has a fundamental growth function, and that life must be accepted and loved as it is. The challenge is to overcome suffering by turning it into joy, as happens in art. Love is a type of alchemical transformation that leads to gold. In earlier times, when human beings lived in direct contact with the divine truths, they did not live amidst so much evil and therefore did not need this process. If we lived a pure life and in direct contact with the divine, pain would not exist. The point of arrival is that where the mind is purified until it re-establishes contact with the absolute self, in order to re-enter as a drop in the ocean.

In my experience, once spiritual energy has been awakened with the help of a true master, it performs the work of purification within us. Awakened energy guides, illuminates and purifies. EFT works on emotional and unconscious blocks in the same way as awakened spiritual energy purifies ancient karmic blocks.

If we want to realize that the feminine is the unconscious, the moon, we must also acknowledge that women have a better capacity to manage the emotional and unconscious dimensions. It is because of this power given to her by God, she can heal and save the world if she follows her nature. Modern women are denying their own power, by competing with that of the male. Woman represents beauty and love. She must regain her spiritual value.

I have written in this book about my therapeutic journey as I have actually lived it, beginning with chaos, and gradually ascending to the light, using all the tools I encountered along the way.

I hope that my narrated experience can help you get closer to truth. And dance it.

13

My Spiritual Guide

So far I have revealed my mystery as a woman and as an artist, telling you all about myself: my body, mind, unconscious, fears, traumas, creative process, relationships, successes and failures, travels, reflections, understandings, sexuality and eroticism. Now I have an even greater ambition—to reveal to you who has been the real inspiration for my life.

I began by telling you that the artist lives in a state of meditation as she creates, but now, I want to take you to the root of the mystery, to the temple of truth. The key to accessing the mystery was, is, and always will be, the heart that longs for love.

I am inviting you to activate this state—the purity of the heart—in going forward with the reading of the story, so that you can understand and experience what you are about to read.

My spiritual guide is a woman who exudes inner beauty and has the power to reawaken that same in anyone who connects with her. Despite being human, she is an instrument of the emanation of divine energy. Her mission is to keep the flame in the heart burning so that she can light it in whoever has the longing for it. She is the light that lights up others' light by transmitting joy.

Meeting such a being is a matter of great fortune. When one is near her, one is imbued with her powerful energy, which nourishes and purifies. One is saved and brought from the darkness of ignorance into the light of knowledge. I am not saying that the journey is easy even after having encountered such a being. Far from it. But I want you to know that even when the game of life makes us pass through dark moments, it is the light she has awakened within us and her presence in our life that make us feel we have been saved.

Understanding her greatness, the spiritual power she possesses that is divine in nature was not easy for me and honestly it is not so, even today. I believe that this can only happen when we have realized the union of the spiritual with the material in ourselves, in which there is no longer any distinction between these two dimensions. Even the great beings, as long as they live in a physical body, are subject to the same rules of physicality as we ordinary mortals are—like growing old and falling ill. Yet they are divine. My spiritual guide has this power, she is a transmitter of great spiritual energy.

How does one find such a being? I feel that on a deeper level, it is her spiritual energy that calls you and helps you to reach her. One is drawn to her based on one's evolution and one's vibration, which matches hers. One can absorb her energy in proportion to how well one's vibrational field can receive her power of attraction.

I believe that the initiation given by the true guru can take place only when we have awakened the will in us to make it happen. It is an intimate and long process which needs to take place in the depths of one's being, which requires its own time, and is different for each one of us.

Spiritual energy guides us based on our karma, our evolution and our efforts. The journey that all of us undertake together with this awakened energy is unique and extraordinary for each one of us.

Each one has their own unique story. I would like everyone to meet a true master who can awaken this energy, which becomes active spontaneously and is free from the one who awakened it. One becomes aware of being the author of everything that happens in life. One is responsible for one's choices whether or not they are in line with the higher Will.

Once the awakening has taken place, it is up to us to feed the fire by throwing in the wood of spiritual practices, personal commitment, introspection, the yearning for the divine, the desire to move forward, to deepen and purify the mind, the unconscious and the body, continually questioning ourselves and others. The spiritual guide, the guru lights the fire, but it is up to us to keep it alive through discipline. I pray to myself, in the form of God, who dwells within me, to be always worthy of remaining connected to her, who is my own inner self.

The divine energy, that is God, is in every cell of the cosmos, and it is clear that if we come into contact with that energy through the heart, we become one with it.

I will try to explain to you what I feel when I am in the heart or in the mind: when I am in the heart, I feel that I am in the right place from which to make my decisions. I perceive an inner smile that reassures me. When I am just in the mind, a sense of anxiety and uncertainty accompanies my thoughts, and I am undecided about the choices to make. Over time I have come to harmonize the heart and mind, to make sure my mind, with all its brilliant capacities is connected to the heart.

After being in India there were long periods of pause and reflection during which I did not do any creative work. I created only when the work had a real reason to exist. At the beginning, I believed that it was India that gave a new light to my existence, that the merit of those experiences belonged solely to that land, famous for its spirituality. Over time I realized that within all this there was an even higher reality, the already active presence in me of not yet aware of, who I later recognized as my spiritual guide.

On my first trip to India I didn't meet her in person but as soon as I arrived I could feel the magic of what was happening to me. One feels one is embraced by spiritual energy, it becomes tangible. I am sure that as soon as I touched the soil of India, she granted me spiritual initiation through her will. The scriptures say that the guru gives initiation in four ways: the will, the gaze, the word and the touch. A real guru awakens spiritual energy that would otherwise remain dormant guiding one from the darkness of ignorance (*gu*) to the light of knowledge (*ru*).

She had drawn me to herself with a call that I always felt within me: the love of God. Her presence has always been in me and was revealed only when I was ready.

God reveals Himself at the right time.

There are two words that she always repeats: respect and love. The West has crushed these values with power, domination and tyranny over Nature.

A year later, during the tour of "C'est ici que l'on prend le bateau", I experienced great pain. I was in love with a dancer, but I refrained from experiencing that overwhelming passion as it scared me. I had dreamed a year before knowing him, of his hands, that as they moved on the piano keyboard, made me feel the love that I would have liked to find, hands that I recognized a few months later, while he was playing in reality.

After the show, while the company went to dinner, I went alone to look at the night from the top of Caserta, crying desperately in the dark, with an excruciating pain in my heart for that relationship from which I had fled. At that moment, I had a cosmic vision of a woman, immense like the infinite, meditating cross-legged, with her eyes closed, black hair and dressed in orange. I heard her voice echoing in and out of me, as she said to me in English: "Infinite ... detachment".

With the voice I felt a deep peace, the same I had experienced only while dancing until then. The pain faded and I rejoined my company at dinner, as if nothing had happened. I behaved like one who wakes up and no longer remembers the dream on coming back into contact with reality. I didn't even wonder what had happened or what that vision had been. Since then, however, I have begun to understand that I was too carried away by emotions which caused me to sink into the abyss of suffering. I should have learned to manage the excessive involvement, soothing it by conquering it with greater detachment. Something not easy to achieve in real life for a passionate woman like me, even if the detachment rises like it does in dance when the body is no longer corporeal. I also believe that we can realize our wishes only when we let go of attachment, and that detachment is the magic key to attract what we desire.

The secret I discovered was that only when there is complete trust in oneself and in the self that insecurity and fear of not being able to achieve what one aspires for, disappears. Only then we realize our wishes. I find detachment. No matter how events evolve it is okay, everything happens for the best.

Although it was a powerful experience, I never talked about that vision even to myself until fourteen years later. It is incredible how the human mind works, how sometimes it veils such overwhelming experiences so as to protect itself. I can testify that the heart always reveals, the mind often conceals.

Ten years after that vision, in May 1989, I actually met her. I was invited to a yoga event in Rome. At that time, a young girl, the daughter of one of my musicians, replaced my secretary who was expecting a baby. Sounding confused she informed me of an invitation received by telephone. What struck me was that the event was taking place at a hotel on the Via Aurelia.

One Sunday, as it often happened, Dino Orlando and I went to Fregene for lunch, and on our way back we passed Ergife Palace Hotel. I remembered that it was the venue and the date on which the Indian yoga event was to take place, but of which I had not understood much. Dino and I decided to take a look since we were there.

From the event poster I gathered that it was a programme featuring a spiritual master from India. My first reaction was annoyance because I had hoped it would be an Indian music concert or a yoga session. A 1968 leftist as I was, I had developed strong anti-religious and more importantly, an anti-guru attitude, so much so that during my travels in India I had always kept well away from all so-called spiritual masters. On that occasion, however, as soon as I entered the room, I felt instantly attracted by the beauty of the people, their brightness, kindness and grace.

Andrea Boni welcomed me warmly and turned out to be the author of that invitation that changed the course of my life.

Among the thousands of people present were notable artists such as Bertolucci and Antonioni. Andrea persuaded me to go in despite my initial resistance, and I found myself in front of her, a woman with a divine presence and extraordinary spiritual power. Her face shone with inner beauty with all the muscles of the face softly radiating an indescribable serenity, and the lips full and generous, similar to Madonna's face in religious images. The power of the light in her enormous, mysterious, deep, sphinx-like eyes, which seemed to pierce through me, intimidated me.

Andrea's father, Cesare Boni, introduced me as a great artist, asking her for a private meeting with me without my having requested it. She granted one though with a puzzled expression on her face, as if she doubted that I really wanted it. I was told that a private meeting was extremely difficult to arrange. As a reaction, I had a vision of a shadow as a figure ten metres tall, which I thought was my ego. It was my fear. I gave up the idea of meeting her out of fear. I was confused and did not know what I could ask, although I had a thousand existential questions inside me that had not yet found answers. I did not even know why I was there; it was purely coincidental. I ran away like hell, out of fear!

In the evening when I returned home I saw a programme by Mino Damato about her on television. Only then did I realize that there was something great that had affected me deeply. Every gesture, look and movement of hers expressed the grace and lightness far superior to that of any great dancer. I fell in love with her.

A few months later, I participated in a video program in which she was the master. I had strong spiritual experiences. Within myself I saw a nocturnal universe made of bright lights and planets, in which I felt that there were no longer borders, between the inside and the outside of me. During meditation, my body, which was sitting cross-legged on the ground, made a movement that I could never have made on my own.

It was the spiritual energy that guided me in an impossible rotation: my back leaned to one side, brushing the floor, my spine turned 45 degree and quickly straightened up while my legs remained motionless as they were. I felt as if a knife came out, from a point on my back where I had always felt a pain, which I have never had again since that moment.

A month later, I was at home, and had an even more incredible experience. As soon as I closed my eyes to prepare for hatha yoga, I had a vision of a dazzling light in the shape of a sesame seed. I was immediately transported into a state of immense love. I felt a strong impulse to open it and to create a passage to dive into that light. But a powerful fear pulled me back and the vision disappeared. What I saw was an indescribable light, a light that people who have had a near-death experience describe. It was the light of thousands of suns.

I discovered that I had had the vision of the Blue Pearl which, according to the sacred texts of India that I studied later, described as being shaped like a sesame seed. It was an experience of overwhelming power, it was as if I had lived for a few moments in the light beyond life. I understood that I had experienced divine love, and that the sesame seed was my immortal self. I could have immersed myself in the light like the drop in the ocean, but I was afraid to do it. I realized that what was happening to me was something mystical, wondrous and indescribable.

That experience gave a new meaning to my life and strengthened my faith. I had no more doubts. What we call God, exists, God is light. God is love.

Soon after that experience, I decided to go to her ashram in India.

One day, in the meditation cave, I heard her voice telling me in English, "Do not go back to Italy, stay here and marry an Indian man, your twin soul."

She mentioned him by his full name.

This message left me completely confused. I came face to face with myself as all the old resistances and fears about the relationship with my soulmate re-emerged.

When I met my soulmate in New York years later, during his concert at Carnegie Hall, I told him about this message. He looked at me in amazement, smiled and replied, "I was told something else," pointing to the sky with an ironic expression, as if to remind me of all the conflicts I had caused between us. He then looked deep into my eyes and added almost reproachfully, "And then, what did you do?"

I retorted, "I called you, but you are never there! How could I have left you a message if the person who answered only spoke Hindi?"

As I already told you, we were married in a dream. For me, experiences lived in dreams are even more intense than those lived in reality, and in cases like this, even satisfying to the point of not feeling the need to realize them concretely. As you can see, I am running away again! Ah-ya-ya ya -ya ya!

Every time I get ready to visit an ashram, something subtle begins to move me. I feel the activation of new energy but at the same time, a kind of accumulated tiredness comes to the surface. The ashram in India is a paradise where every cell is powerfully imbued with divine energy. Everything in this special place is perfect. Everybody is inspired to take care of everything. It is a place of purification, a place to recharge one's batteries, and to experience that every precious moment is part of an intense play of divine Shakti—the universal and creative energy.

Life in this unique place is marked by spiritual practices but one is not obliged to follow them all. However if one manages to do it, something magical happens inside, one gets into a perfect harmony with that energy.

Sacred devotional songs are sung, to the accompaniment of tambura, harmonium, percussion and chorus. Each song has its own arrangement that touches different emotional chords. This practice brings enormous joy and lightness.

Meditation is the most intimate and profound practice for me. I enter the darkness where I find the light, and each time the miracle happens.

Meditating is learning to die, but in the sense that each time a new life is activated, it is the game of fullness and emptiness, of rising and falling, of dynamic stillness and silence that vibrates more than sound itself.

After meditating, I not only feel strong and centred, serene and confident, but I also have the answers and insights I need at that specific moment. It is sufficient to focus attention on the breath and the mantra, for all this to happen spontaneously for those who open themselves to the grace of the guru, as the Principle, the origin of everything.

After the spiritual energy is awakened, the meditation, although intense, occurs naturally and simply. Achieving simplicity is the most difficult thing because it requires purity and humility. It is therefore a process that one must engage with fully. My mind at the beginning starts raising doubts and uncertainties, fears and insecurities, but then focusing on the breath, I become calm and I am able to immerse myself in the space of silence and light. In this way I reconnect to the original source just like when I dance. The most natural meditation for me, you know, has always been to create. The mind gives up, surrenders, it no longer thinks, it becomes a witness of the movement. Only when I dance and meditate am I able to go beyond fear and surrender.

Seva, or selfless service, was the spiritual practice that I learned to appreciate over time because of its purifying effects. The first time I went to the ashram, I was coming out of a period of great work, so I was very tired and needed rest, and I certainly wasn't excited by the idea of continuing to offer my work. I have always lived my profession as service, and with this attitude I offer to humanity what I create, with a sense of profound devotion and gratitude towards the divine, which for me is the mystery of existence.

I avoided this practice of seva and preferred to do all the others, yet every time I participated, I felt a certain sense of well-being afterwards. Offering seva was a challenge because I was forced to interact with others not as a "leader" as I was used to, but like everybody else, as one of the many. It made me see very clearly my difficulties in relating to others.

I can say that seva for me is perhaps the most demanding practice, but it is also one that, in my experience, burns impurities faster, liberating us from the ancient weights that we carry with us and are crushed by. This happens because we offer our work with full love, without feeling that we are the doers. We are only the channel through which the energy does the work.

When I offer seva I express my gratitude, and in return I get a spiritual reward a hundred times greater than the effort I made to give my best. It is an exchange in which love makes you feel at home, but in a cosmic home which unites you with all and the One. A great family in which you and everyone strives spontaneously and generously to offer their best because this is the most beautiful part of the game, it is life itself, when you manage to live it to the fullest.

Over the years, I have done many things as a form of seva, including translating simultaneously for Italians, courses like hatha yoga classes and even my master's talks, along with cleaning tables, laminating photos of the masters, dancing, setting up the rooms, cutting vegetables, welcoming guests from faraway countries, choreographing dance pieces for special occasions and teaching dance.

It doesn't matter what you do in these spiritual places, what matters is how you do it. That is what counts. Whatever I had the honour of being invited to do, I lived it as if it were dancing, letting myself be guided by that special spiritual energy.

A practice that was not easy for me to understand was the offerings of money as an expression of gratitude for all that one is receiving. Only over time did I understand the purity of this spiritual practice because it is like sacrificing material wealth to recognize the spiritual value that supports one's life. This practice comes back to one in double measure.

I was leaving from the ashram to return to Italy when I heard a call to go to visit the goddess of wealth Lakshmi. I had twice as much money as I needed for the taxi fare to the airport, so I went to the image of the goddess to offer the extra amount to her in gratitude.

I immediately went to the reception to call the taxi. Some people who were there were also going to the airport, so they offered me a ride, which I gladly accepted as a blessing and a sign from Goddess Lakshmi. Obviously, these signals arrive if the offerings are made with purity and without expectation of a return because divine consciousness knows everything. Subtle energy moves everything and puts everything at our disposal. It is up to us to make the effort to open ourselves up to welcome it.

I loved walking in the gardens of the ashram where I was staying. There were impressive white statues representing the Hindu gods, the great gurus of history and even Christian saints. My favourite is Lord Ganesh, the elephant-headed god who removes obstacles, and often in meditation with the inner light taking the shape of his eyes and his face. Every thought that emerges from the heart in this precious place is realized. It is a powerful energy that brings you into contact with the mystery. Every thought, emotion, positive or negative, is purified in each cell of one's being in this hallowed place. Truth is beauty they say, but it is purity that makes everything beautiful.

One day in 1993, while staying at an ashram on the East Coast of America, I noticed a photo of my guru in meditation when I entered the room late at night. It was only then, after fourteen years, that the memory of the vision that I had had in Caserta re-emerged, and for the first time I realized that it was really she who had appeared to me then. I recognized her. I fell into deep meditation.

The spiritual awakening given to us by the master puts us in touch with our essence: the self. How amazing is the relationship between the ego and the self!

The ego, the part of us that identifies with the small self or personality, is the factor that creates fear, the fear of God, the fear to surrender to divine love. Suffering is caused by the ego, never by the self. It seems a paradox, the greater the ego the stronger is the potential to overcome it and redirect that strength towards self-realization. I am not afraid of dying but I am afraid of letting go of the opinions and convictions ingrained in me that I have come to be identified with. This is the most difficult attachment to overcome.

Many years ago, my spiritual guide gave talks on how to recognize the ego, its tricks and traps, the dynamics with which it masquerades to maintain power. I was enchanted for hours listening to her. She had a warm, expressive and penetrating voice, which was accompanied with graceful hand gestures. Her long and tapered fingers, her fingertips, eyes and hands make visible the immensity of her unconditional love. During those years, I was in the middle of my psychoanalytic journey, and her talks enriched me with fresh understandings and insights.

Whenever I have had intense experiences of the self, it is as if the ego pulled me back, like an umbilical cord from the world. I recognized that the fear of surrendering myself to the self is in contrast to the certainty of finding myself in it.

It is clear to me that death is similar to the dream state, when the soul detaches itself from the body. The ego remains with the soul in the form of impressions of the lived experiences, which will continue to be activated in subsequent births. The ego can be overcome only when the fire of the spiritual energy, which we nurture with our effort, purifies us from the hold the ego has on us, and keeps us in a contracted state. When the energy purifies all the channels of the flow, then the miracle, the fullness of love, takes place in us.

The embarrassment of the soul in standing naked before God is the last to dissolve; it was not by chance that the first reaction of Adam and Eve was that of embarrassment and shame.

For fourteen years, the ego had veiled the greatness of what had happened in my life, that vision, that voice, "Infinite... Detachment! The real detachment is that of the ego from the soul, it is then that the ego finally dies.

On another of my long stays, I tore the meniscus and she with her infinite compassion, called me. When I went to see her in a wheelchair, she immediately said, "I see that in spite of everything, you smile!"

With love she brought me back to my inner self and I understood that whatever might happen outside, my centre of strength lies in the ability to smile and in the joy of living.

On another occasion, at the end of a two-week retreat, everyone dressed strictly in white, in total silence except for chanting the mantra, we meditated from three in the morning to nine in the evening. She came to give us a talk.

We must have been a thousand people attending the retreat. All of us were purified by those practices, allowing us to enter the heart with ease. Tears flowed out of my eyes as she looked straight at me and said, "These are the tears that wash away the suffering of the world".

I understand the boundary between the microcosm and the macrocosm, the internal and the external worlds, and how to transcend it, but I was rarely able to do so. I understand that when the heart cries, it generates energy that has the power to wash away the pain of the world. These are tears of love that emanate from compassion, the others are tears of the ego that weeps merely because of its own pain.

During another meditation session, she gave everyone in the programme her "touch". It is the guru's way of transmitting spiritual awakening and it was different for each one.

She stroked my cheek gently with her cool, soft fingers and then holding my nape with one hand, pressed me firmly between my eyebrows. I felt an opening of the heart, the breaking of a resistance, and tears began to rush down my cheeks.

I felt pervaded by a sense of profound serenity and surrender, just like when I dance, only I don't cry then.

I stayed in this state for two whole days. I didn't feel the need to eat or sleep, just weep, renewing the deep sense of gratitude which I understand is always connected with love. That is a state of pure joy.

One day in 2013, she took my right hand in hers while pressing my arm with her other hand, and asked me to extend my stay and dance for her. We were in a crowded hall and I had the impression that she was transmitting her energy through her hands to recharge me. At that time,

I had stopped dancing, convinced that I would never return to dance again. She asked me to do it even though I no longer had the desire to.

"Could you dance for me?"

I felt my jaw fall open with astonishment at this request.

Playfully, she added, "Could you extend your stay to dance?"

I realized that she knew that every time I was in her ashrams I could not leave easily, and had always extended my stay for months. Years ago, I would have paid gold to be asked to dance, but my master who is one with the universal consciousness knows everything. Only later, I understood why she gave me so much love by offering me the honour to dance for her.

I think she knew that a few months later I would lose Guido and my mother, and she was giving me the strength to face the circumstances that awaited me. I enthusiastically and spontaneously said, "Yes, but will you dance with me too?"

I will never forget the humble and tender expression with which she said, "Oh no, no, no, but I will be an excellent spectator."

I insisted, "Dance with me, you are the greatest dancer I have ever seen."

She then turned to Enrico Bisante, who was close to me, and asked him, "Are you a dancer too?"

Enrico replied pointing out, "No, I'm an eye doctor!"

She asked him why he had changed the photo of his name tag.

Enrico showed her the old photo from fourteen years before. It showed a striking change in his face over the years. She laughed. As he looked slightly embarrassed, she said, "But now you are more beautiful! Your eyes are as beautiful as Omar Sharif's!" After taking a few steps away she turned unexpectedly and added, "Bye-bye, Omar Sharif!"

Enrico's mother used to tell everyone from the time he was a child, that Omar Sharif had eyes like Enrico's! He confided in me that at that moment he felt the immense love of the master like that of a mother. Today Enrico is dancing with me in celebration of the precious collaboration on the final draft of this book.

On the same occasion she also told a German girl to do "tapping" with me to overcome her snake phobia. She knew that I used EFT without anyone telling her. Such beings are one with the universal consciousness and this is why they know everything. The sole purpose of their every word and action is to guide us in our spiritual growth.

For each of us, she is a mirror that sends us the image of who we are, capturing our different facets and nuances, and guiding us to realize ourselves in shaping our soul. She asked us to be disciplined in our spiritual practices. Over the years, I have been able to see that all my friends on this path have learned from her to take care of the details in their work and to have respect for their collaborators. They are in fact professionals of the highest quality.

It was a great emotional experience and an honour to prepare to dance for her and everyone else at the ashram. It was as if she had put all the joy and pain as a woman and an artist into a blender and mixed them to raise me up in a powerful experience. It was unbelievably intense.

The evening before the performance, during dinner time when everyone was present, she arrived, announcing herself from far away, with her echoing laughter, a nectar that nourishes and unleashes a sparkling joy. When she came near the table where I was having dinner with many other friends, she said loudly as if into a megaphone: "Patrizia! Are you ready to dance tomorrow?"

"Sure!" I replied with equal vigour.

What an exceptional promotion! The next day I was not surprised to see a full house.

On my first trip to India in 1979, I performed the solo of the hands, which is a piece from my production, *Tendrils*. In this, I am seated cross-legged on the floor and expressing/interpreting the music with only my hands. It was she who inspired me. I also interpreted the theme of "C'est ici que l'on prend le bateau" (This is the place where we take the boat). I had the honour of being accompanied on the piano in an improvisation by Kenny Werner, a passionate jazz musician from America.

At the end of the performance, during the applause, I embraced the musicians and then ran with the spontaneity of a little girl to embrace her as well. Some of the spectators told me that I had dared to do what many of them would have liked to, but didn't have the courage to. Embrace her!

When she invited the audience to share their thoughts on the performance, a ten-year-old girl said, "I was very impressed, especially by the technical skills and precision of the movements. Patrizia should never stop dancing."

My Master added, "She is an example of discipline and how you should do anything. Of course, she must *also* continue to dance. In some moments, Patrizia expressed melancholy in her dance, transforming it into joy, because she knows how to process and transform emotions. When we see her dancing, it seems as if the whole cosmos is dancing with her."

It is true. For me, discipline is my strength; it is the best way to contain the energy that would otherwise dissipate inexorably, dispersing in the fatuity of life. Discipline enriches life because it uses energy to the fullest without wasting it, directing it where it is needed, allowing you to give your best. It is what each of us wants to do, as it is the only way to feel fulfilled and happy.

The word she used "also", has opened up new horizons. The power of the word of such a spiritual master reverberates within you and guides you in achieving all that is in your destiny, in accordance with the divine plan. I must not only dance, but *also* live all the other aspects of life.

At the luncheon that followed the event, she approached the table where we were seated, along with everyone else who had worked on the show, including artists and technicians. Standing majestically, she said that the dance had inspired her to start activities dedicated to bodily expressiveness, and she said this by joining hands with us all, as happens in the final part of that choreography. I realized that just as God inspires us, we also inspire God. Isn't it wonderful?

She wanted the head of the hatha yoga department to organize my dance classes. I was also invited to create five different dance sequences of ten-minute duration for all ashramites. Each session had to be expressive, with creative, rhythmical, pleasant and enjoyable movements that anyone, whether a child or a ninety-year-old could perform. It was a big challenge for me, much more difficult than choreographing for professional dancers! But it was well worthwhile. Everyone looked so happy and invigorated after the session.

I recall that on another occasion, everyone had been sent to lunch but I was made to stay back with those who were leaving that day. I was invited to sit down in a spot of the hall right where she would pass by. As she approached, I got up and lost myself in her deep eyes, with the feeling of respect and love that always arises in those who look at them. As she passed me she said, "But how are you still here, didn't you go to the Italian table?"

I replied firmly and courageously, without any shyness or modesty, in a loud voice, "I prefer to stay with you."

While I watched from behind her as she moved ahead, majestic and cheerful, I had the impression that she was pleased with what I had announced.

I am telling you about this incident to make you a part of the reflections that her words sparked in me. I felt as if she wanted me to clarify my doubts about whether or not to leave Italy. I still can't cut the umbilical cord with my country, from which, however, I continue to take every opportunity to escape. The first and last time I asked her if I should go back to Italy or stay with her, she turned her head away and without looking at me, said, "If it is convenient!" Later, I realized that no matter where you are, being with the guru means maintaining connection, in thoughts, dreams, emotions and nurturing joy through spiritual practices.

I contemplate everything she has told me over the years and the answers that emerge are still enriching me. I also know that I will never cease to understand her messages because, like symbols, they contain truths that will never cease to reveal themselves fully.

My dears, when such a spiritual master speaks to you there is something very profound to process. Her mission is to do everything necessary to guide us in finding our answers within ourselves.

She is always present within me and I am sure that her beneficial, healing energy flows through me to all those I meet. I consider myself one of the souls that belong to her. She saved me and is gradually leading me increasingly into the state of inner freedom. I am grateful for this and I hope I will never stop being so. It is in gratitude that we find ourselves naked before God, surrendered in truth.

In the presence of such a being, one is filled with unconditional love and understanding that love is not a feeling, it is a state of being.

Meeting my guru was my greatest fortune and the best gift I received in life.

Have I succeeded in transmitting to you the greatness of God, which manifested itself in my life through the presence of such a guru?

Thank you for wanting to dance with me.

Love,

Pat

Acknowledgements

My heartfelt thanks to:

Sukrita Paul Kumar for believing in this book even before reading it and supporting it based on her trust in my value as an artist and a woman. She has added her poetical touches to both the English and Hindi editions.

Patrizia Macagno my assistant and friend who immensely helped in writing this book as she did with my dance and my EFT workshops.

Enrico Bisante for using his great sensitivity as a reader and suggesting a better assembly of the parts and a deepening of the themes developed.

Luigi Troiani for encouraging me to write this book, helping in finalizing the main title of the book and working with me on it.

Sanjoy Roy for fine-tuning the main title of the book.

Keerti Ramachandra for her passion, sensitivity and talent in translating this English edition and using her intuition in the choice of every word and expression.

Aditi, Vani Prakashan books, India, for publishing my book for the very first time in Hindi.

Smita Mishra Chaturvedi for enthusiastically translating the book into Hindi.

Cesare Paris for transcribing the interviews and giving his feedback in the process.

Elena Romeo for delving deep into the process with me.

De Luca Editori d'Arte, Luigi and *Stefano* for publishing the Italian edition of this book.

Jyotsna Mehta, senior editor of Om Books International, for immensely enriching the text of this English edition with her precious inputs.

Shantanu Ray Chaudhuri, chief editor of Om Books International, for readily accepting the proposal to publish the book.

Photo Credits

Cristiano Cataldo
Giovanni Catalano
Roberto Cavanna
Corrado Maria Falsini
Roberto Ferrantini
Cristina Ghergo
Guido Paolo Menocci
Sebastiana Papa